Praise for David Atkins and
The One Decision Away Philosophy

"David didn't let the boiling water change him – he changed the water. His life, his work, and this book are a blueprint for becoming the kind of person who doesn't just survive the heat ... but thrives in the heat."

> – Damon West, 3X Wall Street Journal
> bestselling author of *The Coffee Bean*

"'Do your best and forget the rest' has been my mantra for years – and David Atkins is a walking example of what that really means. In *The One Decision Away Philosophy*, he brings clarity, heart, and no-nonsense guidance to help you make the kind of decisions that lead to real transformation. Fueled by passion and purpose, David shows you that change doesn't come all at once. It comes one powerful decision at a time!"

> – Tony Horton, creator of P90X,
> fitness professional, author

"David Atkins delivers a masterclass in intentional living. *The One Decision Away Philosophy* isn't just a book – it's a blueprint for anyone ready to take full responsibility for their life, their goals, and their future. If you lead people, run a business, or want to step into your next level, this book is a non-negotiable read."

> – Anthony Trucks, former NFL athlete,
> Identity Shift Coach, founder of Dark Work

"David Atkins is an absolute go-getter and a high performer who has inspired me with his uncompromising work ethic to truly live his life intentionally. Not only is David a powerful motivational speaker, capable of bringing audiences to tears while simultaneously inspiring them to change their lives in the best ways, but he's real, raw, and authentic to his core. In *The One Decision Away Philosophy*, he distills his most valuable life-enriching principles into palatable, bite-size action steps that we can all incorporate into our busy lives. Learn how to cultivate a life well-lived, on your terms, by following David's example. You're one decision away from living your life intentionally, to create your best self."

— Joe Gagnon, ultra-endurance athlete, CEO,
and author of *Living Intentionally*

"Reading this book is in itself a great decision! We created *'Decide. Commit. Succeed.'* as our tagline at Beachbody (now BODi) to empower people to achieve lasting lifestyle change by starting with *the decision* to prioritize their health, fitness, and overall well-being. Making that decision is what takes the inconsistent variable of motivation out of the equation. "You decided. Now follow through." David captures the power of that sentiment so well in both his book and in his speaking engagements. And in the same way he has helped thousands of people achieve incredible health transformations and achieve their potential in any endeavor, he is now scaling his insights to teach the power of being decisive in life with this powerful book."

— Carl Daikeler, CEO/Co-Founder,
BODi, formerly Beachbody

"David Atkins reminds us that we're never as far from the life we want as we think we are — we're just one decision away. This book is the wake-up call that so many of us need to stop waiting and start *choosing* with intention. David's powerful storytelling and wisdom inspire us to take ownership of our paths, embrace growth through action, and lead with purpose. A fantastic read for anyone ready to level up their life."

— Ella Magers, MSW; Holistic Fitness Coach,
author, host, founder, EllaMagers.com

"I absolutely love the message behind *The One Decision Away Philosophy*. This book is a powerful reminder that the life we want is always just one intentional choice away. As a wellness entrepreneur, author, and founder of Xtend, I've built my life around purposeful action and the importance of staying aligned with purpose, discipline, and daily action — exactly what this book inspires. David's words are both motivating and practical, and his philosophy resonates deeply with anyone striving for more. I highly recommend this to anyone ready to elevate their life."

— Andrea Leigh Rogers., founder
Xtend Barre & author

"Before his books and motivational speaking career, I witnessed firsthand how David's attitude and faith can propel one through life's most difficult obstacles. In my time as Championship Director with the United States Golf Association (USGA), during preparations for the 2020 U.S. Open at Winged Foot Golf Club, I was fortunate in my life to cross paths with a certain New York State Police officer, Captain David Atkins. David was appointed Incident Commander of the U.S. Open, representing New York State Police and working together with the USGA to ensure the safety of a globally recognized sporting event. Given the year 2020, this particular event was a significant milestone in the sports world, demonstrating how a major event could adapt to the challenges posed by the COVID-19 pandemic, while maintaining the integrity of the competition and safety of the community.

I am often asked how this championship was conducted in the same county (Westchester) that was considered one of our country's earliest and most significant epicenters of the pandemic. Some even share that a book should be written on how. Well, good news, the answers in so many ways point to the powerful principles in this book.

David Atkins' embodiment of living what he speaks, accompanied by his relentless discipline and no excuses lifestyle, is a refreshing message that manages to cut through the noise and clutter of today's social media self-help algorithm. He's real, he's relatable, and speaks with a humility of sharing his own struggles, even his own doubts. His story, while inspiring, is also a masterclass in how to take ownership of your life, instilling a belief that wherever you are on your journey, and whatever obstacle you're facing, you're truly just one decision away. Over the years, David has felt moved to share the challenges he's faced and the many one-time decisions that aided him in navigating the proverbial forks in the road. With *The One Decision Away Philosophy*, I'm grateful David has unlocked his playbook for turning dreams into reality …. No secrets. No frills. Just a determination to stack days and a faith that hard work pays dividends. His friendship continues to inspire me to make the one decision to show up every day with my faith, for myself, my health, my family, and my career."

– Charlie Howe, COO, Beemok
Sports & Entertainment

"I had the privilege of hearing David speak at the Ohio Association of Chiefs of Police Conference in Columbus, Ohio. I left that conference with a completely different attitude about family, faith, work, and life in general. I could not get home fast enough to start reading his book *The Leveled Up Life*."

David is highly energetic and is a genuine person who truly cares about people. He is a man who deeply loves his family and is willing to step out of his comfort zone to chase his dreams. Anyone, or any organization who has the chance to hear David speak should not miss that opportunity.

The One Decision Away Philosophy will be a valuable tool to help with fears of failure, self-control, gratitude for the things that you have, your family, and life in general.

I have recommended the book *The Leveled Up Life* to all of our staff. We have used it as part of the study material for promotional processes. I will highly recommend *The One Decision Away Philosophy* as it will also be added to the recommended reading for our staff."

– Richard D. Hines, Chief of Police,
Mariemont Police

"I can't tell you how pleased I was to be asked to endorse Dave's new book. Frankly, my connection to Dave is one of failure. During the COVID-19 crisis, the New York State Police were called upon to solve logistical and organizational challenges, in addition to providing public safety in a dangerous and turbulent time. I was new in a leadership role when I first had a chance to work closely with then-Captain Atkins. I ran into a major issue/problem and promptly processed to panic. A colleague at the time told me to relax, we will just have Dave Atkins handle this ... problem, major logistical problem solved. And he was nice about it at a time when panic and stress were the order of the day. It would be too simple to say he did it with a smile on his face, it was more than that; it was a positive attitude on steroids. Every encounter I had with him after that reinforced that impression. I marked him for immediate promotion. But much to the benefit of folks Dave has come into contact with in his new life, and much to my dismay, David moved on to new challenges, but always with an eye to helping others. The Troopers' loss is your gain as a reader of this inspirational and joyful book."

— Kevin Bruen, New York State
Police Superintendent

"In *The One Decision Away Philosophy*, David Atkins shows us the transformative power of each moment of life. We can either drift along, wondering and worrying about our circumstances, or embrace the truth of life, that each moment carries with it the potential for growth and transformation.

It is true that one decision can change everything for the better, and this truth gives us faith in what is possible for ourselves and for society. Beyond philosophy and principles, the book also has a practical and powerful array of tactics that can be used by anyone aspiring for growth, to use in service of transcending limitation and more fully embracing the miracle of each moment of life. Do yourself a favor and embrace this book and be inspired to do the same with each moment of your life."

— Ravi Raman, executive coach
and entrepreneur

"*The One Decision Away Philosophy* strips away the noise and gets right to the heart of transformation. David's honest, down-to-earth approach will motivate you—but more importantly, it will equip you. Change doesn't have to be overwhelming – it just takes one decision, and David will show you how.

This book reminds us that progress doesn't require perfection – it just requires movement. David gives you the mindset and tools to take that next powerful step."

– Tim Kaufman, founder of FatMan Rants,
motivational speaker, and author of *Escape:
Breaking Free from a Self-Made Prison*

"Every day is a new decision. David Atkins forcefully and fearlessly reminds us that we are just 'one decision away' from changing our lives. After the loss of his best friend, a fellow New York State Trooper, David made his decision: to live his life with purpose. In *The One Decision Away Philosophy*, David gives us the courage to make the right decisions in our own lives. A better life is just one decision away."

– Colin A. Burns, General Manager,
Winged Foot Golf Club, 1991-2022

"Self-reflection alone can be difficult. However, actually solving a problem of your own or 'figuring it out' is unlikely, at best. Further, being able to articulate that solution to the aid of helping others is phenomenal. That's what David Atkins has done in this book. He didn't think outside the box; he broke it. David figured out a life-lesson that is applicable across every area of your existence – and kept it simple – make *one* decision. His kindness resonates throughout the pages of impactful stories, while he took the time and care to develop actionable exercises, to challenge and champion you to achieve personal results.

If you want to pursue greatness, but hesitate with uncertainty of your personal potential, then read and apply these tools for some clarity, reassurance and self-encouragement.

If you make one decision today, it should be to read this book."

— David Lee Jensen, Fortune 50 speaker,
2X bestselling author, CEO coach

THE

ONE
DECISION
AWAY

PHILOSOPHY

THE

ONE DECISION AWAY

PHILOSOPHY

ONE DECISION CAN CHANGE EVERYTHING

DAVID ATKINS

ISBN 979-8-9862869-3-8 (Hardback)
ISBN 979-8-9862869-4-5 (Paperback)
ISBN 979-8-9862869-5-2 (e-Book)
ISBN 979-8-9862869-6-9 (Audio Book)

First Printing

Editor: Grace Catton
Cover and Interior Design and Layout:
    kimmontefortebookdesign.com

For Kristen, my wife and my
rock through this entire journey.
For Cassidy, Sadie, and Addison,
my inspiration daily to always
be my best. Love you all.

Contents

Foreword

David Atkins is a straight shooter, a high performer, and a man on a mission to help others tap into their full potential. The moment I was introduced to David, I knew he was the real deal. Not just because I was connected to David by a mutual friend who is a fellow author and high-performer, but David revealed himself to be a down to earth, principled, high achiever who is always smiling and looking for the best in every situation. That's the perception I had of David upon meeting him. Knowing that he's a husband, a father, a former police captain, a fitness enthusiast, and a man of faith, I anticipated David's friendliness, warmth, and strong character. Even the fact that I can't always reach him by text or email on weekends, because he is dedicated to spending his time with his wife and daughters to build an enriching life, tells me what I need to know about David's character.

When I read *The One Decision Away Philosophy*, I got to know David even better. I learned about his experiences that have shaped his worldview, his struggles, his achievements, and his aspirations for himself and for his family. As you read this book, you will also get to know David, but you'll likely get to know yourself a lot better too. David asks us to discover our why, our purpose, our goals and our visions for the future, but also asks us to recognize the obstacles, barriers, and habits that are holding us back. You're one decision away from the life you envision for yourself. Will you have faith in yourself and in your future to make the leap?

As I reflect back on my own decisions in life – those moments that define who I am today – I am reminded that I too was just one decision away from one outcome or another, depending on whether I took action or sat on the sidelines. Many of us have an identity that we resonate with or which others know us by. For me, that's being a vegan athlete. As I like to say, I've been vegan since the late nineteen hundreds (since 1995). I grew up on a farm, raised farmed animals who were like pets, and I was their best friend, and then I sold them in an auction to be turned into someone's meal. Upon recognizing my own hypocrisy, turning my back on the animals who trusted me more than anyone else in the world, I decided to become a vegan, avoiding the consumption or exploitation of animals, and I have lived that way ever since. I was only 15 years old at the time, barely weighing over 100 pounds as a five-sport athlete in high school, and I had no idea that on December 8th, 1995, that one decision I made to become vegan would change my life forever. It was the same year the internet was coming of age, and many of us got computers to learn how to use this new concept of a World Wide Web. I had to carve out my own path with limited resources to learn what to eat, and how to live, especially as a 5-sport athlete, since Google wasn't even invented yet.

That one decision I made led me to becoming the world's most recognized vegan bodybuilder for more than a decade, embarking on a speaking tour for the past 21 years, writing six books on the topic, including the *New York Times* best-seller, *The Plant-Based Athlete*, and enabled me to tour around the world sharing my story of transformation from skinny farm kid to champion vegan bodybuilder. My success in my field, from that one decision, opened up so many other doors. It led to other decisions, like the one to change from being an endurance runner to a bodybuilder, which is where I made my name known. I grew from weighing 120 pounds to 220 pounds over the years, en route to landing on numerous magazine covers and showing the world a completely new perspective of what it meant to be a "vegan athlete." I made the decision to be a speaker on a vegan cruise, even though at the time, I could barely afford my airfare from Oregon to Florida, which is where I met my wife more than 14 years ago. We've been back on that cruise together every year since, and rather than struggling to afford the trip, it is completely complimentary for me and my wife, and I am paid well as a presenter on board, year after year. Even outside of my vegan identity, which is what I'm internationally known for, I made plenty of other decisions that at the time seemed fairly insignificant, but later on, I would realize that they changed the trajectory of my life. One of those decisions, to embrace a brand new career as a book writing consultant after publishing my own books for more than 15 years, is what led me to David through our mutual friend, and fellow author, Joe Gagnon.

Just a few months before this writing, I had no idea that I would become a writing consultant. I was already nearing the end of my seventh book when I accepted an opportunity that fell into my lap. And now I am having the best time ever, supporting other established and aspiring writers to bring their stories to life, helping them make their dreams come true. I couldn't have anticipated this outcome, but I was one decision away from where I am right now, doing what I love, because I made the decision to serve others. I always believed that I needed to write for myself, but once I realized that I could use my skills, talents, and network to write for others, and support their goals, it became even more rewarding than penning another book for myself. I've shared my story, as a reminder that we all have our own one decision away stories, even if we haven't thought about them or given them the attention they deserve. When you reflect back on the turning points in your life, what decisions opened up new doors for you, and what made you step forward and walk through them?

In *The One Decision Away Philosophy*, David outlines his own system of principles to follow, based on his lived experiences from climbing the ranks as a New York State Trooper, becoming a police captain, managing an entire county in one of the most populated states in the country, to growing a million-dollar business from the ground up, while wiping away six-figures in debt, to becoming a highly sought-after motivational speaker for fortune 500 companies. Over the course of 24 chapters, David lays the groundwork for what it takes to have the mindset to make the tough decisions, to have the hard conversations, with yourself, or with others, and to overcome obstacles that will inevitably show up along the way. As warm as David is, he also shares some tough love with us about some of the habits that are holding us back. Perhaps that's the police officer in him, teaching us what we might not even realize about ourselves, or the entrepreneur in him that built a seven-figure business with a team of 1,400. He has a tried and true real-world lived experience, and he's sharing some mistakes he made along the way, so that we can learn from him, and avoid those for ourselves.

I encourage you to read *The One Decision Away Philosophy* with an open mind and with an open heart. I am eternally grateful for some of the most important decisions I made in my life – the ones that truly defined me and provided me with some of life's most wonderful experiences – and my goal is that you too will lean into life-changing decisions that put you on the path to becoming the best version of yourself. Whatever your goals are, whatever your aspirations for your future may be, David reminds us that we're all just one decision away from living our best life. So, what decision do you need to make in your life right now? What have you been holding back? Who do you want to be? How do you want to show up in the world? When will you decide to step into your greatness and become the person that you're meant to be? You're just one decision away from revealing your answer. May you embrace the change you long for, and become the person that is waiting to be unleashed. You have it in you, and you're just one decision away from your incredible future self. Take action, and make your dreams happen.

— Robert Cheeke, *New York Times* bestselling coauthor of *The Plant-Based Athlete*

Introduction

t's been about 2 years since I wrote *The Leveled Up Life* and spoke to thousands of people as their keynote speaker. I was often asked if I would write another book. My answer was always quite simple: "Not right now, but you never know." Internally, I had a much deeper thought process going on.

First, I still enjoyed the book signings and the message I shared in *The Leveled Up Life*. It took many years of growth, maturity, and, I guess, aging (ugh!) to realize that we need to strive to enjoy the present moments and learn to simply be where our feet are. Too many of us let life pass us by because we are always looking at what's next. We ask ourselves: "What should I do next?" "What is my next goal?" "When I reach that goal, I will be happy!" "When I do this, I can finally take a break." But often, we don't even realize that life is passing us by. Instead, we must understand it's the journey we are currently in that we need to focus on. That's where we need to find happiness. Happiness is not something you can chase, but rather it's about finding it in the moments we are presently in.

Second, I have learned throughout my life to always look for signs or at my intuition to guide me. My friend and successful business entrepreneur Moira Kucaba likes to say,

"Listen to the whispers! LTTW." I love that! For me, it has to be something in my heart that I know feels right. I may not feel prepared to take that next step, but when I wake up each day with a new little butterfly feeling in my belly, then that's a sign I need to pay attention to. It's telling me I am onto something, and that I may be *one decision away* from something big. I wasn't having this feeling yet, and writing a book cannot be forced. I cannot force the innovation, creativity, or message I want to share.

If we can focus on being the happiest, healthiest, most confident, hard-working people we can be, then the rest will reveal itself to you. I cannot worry about what I will do 3 months from now. I must focus on being better today than I was yesterday and have the faith that new doors will open for me. This has always held tried and true throughout my life.

So here I am in the spring of 2024, and I have been getting messages from a fellow keynote speaker who I thought was trying to sell me on his coaching services. At this point in my speaking career, I have already hired a few coaches to help me both get started and improve my presentation, so I was quick to respond, "Thank you, but I am all set." To my surprise, the person wrote back and actually explained to me that we speak for similar associations, and that they would love to connect and get to know each other. At first, I was hesitant to get on a call out of fear it would take me away from something else more important, but I also know networking and getting to know other speakers is essential. I once heard that "your network is your net worth." This was something I believed in, so knowing I had nothing to lose, I decided to make the *one decision* and get on a call with this fellow speaker.

We had a great conversation on Zoom, and at the end of our call, he said to me, "David, I want to recommend this book to you. It was recommended to me, and I want to share it with you. It's called *The Referable Speaker.*" He explained how easy it was to read and how powerful the information in the book was. We said our goodbyes, thank yous, and hung up. I was grateful that we had our call and thought to myself how easily I could have avoided it, but I was glad I made the *one decision* not to.

I ordered the book and it arrived the same day I was getting ready to travel to South Carolina to speak to a company of a few hundred property managers. I wasn't anticipating this, but when the book arrived, I immediately felt anxious about reading it. Why? I spent a lot of time preparing my presentation for the event I had the following day and felt ready to deliver my message. However, simultaneously, I knew if I started reading that book, it may completely derail my mindset because I was sure there would be something in there that I would want to add. The tension I felt internally about this book I almost cannot describe. It made me feel sick. I remember packing my suitcase in my bedroom, looking at the book next to the bed, and walking away multiple times. I don't know what overcame me, but at some point, I made the *one decision* to place it in my bag.

When I arrived at La Guardia Airport and went to the Delta Sky Lounge to get something to eat (because I had about an hour to kill), that butterfly feeling came over me again. But this time, it was about whether I should start reading the book.

I want to stop here for a quick second and share something I have learned throughout my life growing as a speaker, entrepreneur, life coach, the ranks of the state police and even as a husband and father to three girls. When you have that feeling in your gut, like I am describing above, and you know in your heart it's something you need to face, this is a compelling sign to make that *one decision* and lean into it. This is precisely where you need to be. This is not a stop sign in your life. This is a growth sign. That tension you feel is God's way of pulling your life to the next level. Too many people stop right here. I knew I was potentially *one decision away* from something that could catapult my life forward as a keynote speaker. So, what did I do as nervous as I was? Faith over fear, my friends. I took the book out of my bag and began reading as I ate my lunch in the Delta Sky Lounge. I thought to myself, "What did you get yourself into David? You're speaking in less than 12 hours. Are you really going to do this to yourself?" Then, with a little more conviction I thought, "Yes, I am."

I couldn't put the book down. I took out my highlighter and began marking up all sorts of key points in the book. I read it for an hour straight as I waited to board the plane, and other than the time it took to walk to the gate and get seated on the plane, I continued to read. Nonstop. For the entire ... 3 ... hour ... plane ... ride. When we landed, I quickly exited and grabbed my luggage. When I got in my Uber to the hotel, I continued to read, even though reading in the car made me nauseous. I got to the hotel, checked in, and even continued to read in my room. I was relentless and ultimately did something I never do. I finished the book from start to finish on the same day. This was saying something. Don't get me wrong, I am always reading books that interest me, but I never picked one up and finished it on the same day. This is what happened next.

Something hit me as I sat in my hotel room, thinking about the book and how it could improve my current presentation.

It created so many different emotions inside of me because it both had me thinking about so many ways I could make my presentation better, but at the same time it generated a sense of urgency to act quickly on my new thoughts. So first, let me explain a significant part of the book. The book talks about combining both transformation and entertainment in your keynote presentation. To transform the audience not just by "*what* you share" and giving just a "*how-to*" speech, but rather giving a "*how-to-think*" speech. When this happens, it becomes "transformational" in someone's life. If you can do that and pair it with an entertainment factor, you deliver an unforgettable keynote. The main title of my message up until now has always been "No Excuses." That is the what of my message. No more excuses. I still live and believe in that today. But what about the "*how-to-think*" part? It then hit me. Every single aspect of my life where I was successful always came down to *one simple decision* I made that was always right in front of me. That *one decision* has always led to the next chapter in my life. I was always *one decision away* from something that changed the direction of my life for the better. Getting on a call with that fellow speaker was *one decision away* at that very moment. That *one decision* led me to get this book. Getting that book led to the *one decision* to start reading it. The *one decision* to start reading gave me the epiphany that when we get over our excuses, we are all only *one decision away* from changing our lives for the better. This realization scared the heck out of me. When I look back at my life (I will discuss more later in this book), it was the numerous decisions I made that were always only *one decision away* from me that led to where I am today. This blew my mind. Yes, my message will always be about helping people get over their excuses, and I will always continue to focus on vision, mindset, and living with a sense of urgency in your life. However, everyone must realize no matter what their past has been, we are all only *one decision away* from facing that fear, having that vision again, changing our mindset for the better, not procrastinating anymore, and understanding we often overcomplicate our lives. Keep it simple. You are *one decision away* from moving your life forward. That is how you need to think, and in a matter of a day, through this *one decision,* my keynote just became transformational.

I didn't wait to start sharing this epiphany I just had. I immediately started bread crumbing the "One Decision Away" phrase that very next day throughout my keynote presentation, and to no surprise, it stuck! How did I know? During my book signing after my presentation, people approached me saying, "David, one decision away! I got it!" This blew my mind. What just happened? How did this happen? After that event, I sat in my hotel room silently and felt I was onto something big. The more I thought about it, the more I realized that I have been applying this philosophy without even knowing it my entire life. Then, when I inserted it into my presentation, it fit like a glove; people loved it, and more ideas started flowing.

Remember above when I shared that people would often ask me about my next book and whether I would write one? I often answered, "Not right now, but you never know." Well, after this event, not only did I know I was onto something, but I realized this was a sign. A sign that it was time to write another book. As I sat in this hotel full of emotions, my next book was just *one decision away* from happening, and here we are. Welcome to a philosophy that can alter your life's direction, as it has for thousands of others and me since I began sharing the idea just a few months ago. I cannot wait to share more about it with you, how to apply it, and the obstacles that will come and try to get in your way.

CHAPTER 1

What Exactly Is the One Decision Away Philosophy?

So now that I have shared with you how the One Decision Away philosophy came to be, the first question that may come to mind is, what exactly is it? What is the One Decision Away philosophy? This is how I define it: *"It's a choice made in the present moment backed by courage and faith to move you one step closer to your goals."*

Note how I said, *"Backed by courage and faith."* I think it's important to discuss these two specific points before I go any further. As simple as the One Decision Away philosophy is, we humans tend to overcomplicate things constantly. We make mountains out of molehills. We live in the past. We worry about too many things even though the vast majority of things we worry about never actually come to pass. But all this worrying ultimately leads to more worrying unless we take action. Taking action can lead to results, while worrying leads us to nothing.

First, let's talk about courage. The underlying obstacle of what I briefly described above comes down to fear. No matter who you are, we all face fear at some point in our lives. Fear of failure. Fear of success. Fear of judgment. (I will be discussing this further in this book.) We all have fear. No one is immune to it, and our brains are wired to protect us. In what our bodies deem as a life-and-death situation, fight or flight syndrome always kicks in. But far too often, especially today, we run away from something because our brain thinks it needs to protect us when, in fact, it has nothing to do with a life-and-death situation. Remember, when facing all of the things you have feared up until this point you have a success rate of 100 percent. Why? Because you are still here. You survived everything up until now. So, it takes one simple word to face our fears: courage. Having the courage to face our fears allows us to take action, make that *one decision,* and put ourselves on track to live up to our fullest potential. Far too many people let fear stop them. We sit and wait until we feel ready. The truth is we will never feel ready. We must learn to have the courage to make that *one decision* that can change our lives.

Next, let's talk about faith. Something I will also be discussing more about later on in this book. But it's important

IT'S A CHOICE MADE IN THE PRESENT MOMENT BACKED BY COURAGE AND FAITH TO MOVE YOU ONE STEP CLOSER TO YOUR GOALS.

to touch on it now since it is a big part of the One Decision Away philosophy. I like to say faith is the belief in things you cannot see. In the Bible, Hebrews 11:1 says, *"Now faith is the assurance of things hoped for, the conviction of things not seen."* So, when it comes to making that *one decision,* we need both faith and courage to make it. We are not meant to know the outcome. We will never know the outcome before we act. That's where faith comes in. Additionally, we must remember that even if we hit obstacles along the way (which we always will), we must have faith that we will always learn something from that obstacle and that we can make the next decision to move us forward. We cannot sit still.

When I look back on my life, it has been a series of single decisions that have brought me to where I am today. In the introduction, I mentioned how scared I was when the One Decision Away philosophy came to me, and this is why. When I was 12, I wanted to get a batting cage in my backyard, and little did I know that the *one decision* to accept a job as a newspaper delivery boy taught me life skills such as consistency, discipline, perseverance, grit, and vision. Then, when I *decided* to pursue being an ocean lifeguard in college, I developed a stronger sense of those same principles but also learned what it meant to have courage and faith because I feared failing. When I made the *one decision* to become a state trooper and leave college during my senior year (seriously, who does that?!), all these principles came into play, and I had no idea the life events that I would experience and the opportunities that would be presented to me that would change my life forever. Then, when I made the *one decision* to become a network marketer with Beachbody and build a business, little did I know the *one decision* I made when I was 12 to accept a newspaper route, the *one decision* I made to become an ocean lifeguard, and the *one decision* to become a state trooper would all prepare me to build a business that had so much negativity surrounding it. Now, follow this closely, if it weren't for all these single decisions I made throughout my life, I wouldn't have been in the position to be asked to share my story and speak in front of about 15 people, which then opened the door to where I am today as a keynote motivational speaker traveling the country and speaking to thousands. I learned all the life skills of grit, perseverance, discipline, consistency, and vision. Throughout my life, I have always been *one decision away* from something that would impact my life in a positive way years later.

I also need to bring something vital to your attention. We are not meant to understand how everything will fall into place in the future. I did not know that what I did at 12 would impact me at 47. It's impossible to predict our future. The main point of the One Decision Away philosophy is that you make whatever decision you need today to improve your life.

MAKING NO DECISION IS A DECISION.

It's not about the decision you will make next week. You need to make the first single decision today. Furthermore, this also can work in the exact opposite way. If you fail to make the decisions to move your life forward, well, that's also a decision too.

Making no decision is a decision. If you are not where you want to be or find yourself in a pretty bad place, it is probably because you procrastinated and made excuses for the decisions you knew you needed to make. It works both ways. So, if you were to look back at your life, you can probably identify all the decisions you made or didn't make to bring you to where you are today. We are all a product of the choices and decisions we made up until this point. Don't worry if you aren't happy with where you are today. You can always apply the One Decision Away philosophy to improve your life.

People too often worry about all the correct steps necessary to reach their goals, but truthfully, it's about making the *one decision* that's right in front of you. Life will then reveal your next step to you. So stop trying to figure out what you must do next week or the week after. You are *one decision away* from what you need to do today. Start there! I often say work with what you have, with where you are, because what you have is plenty. Stop worrying about steps 2, 3, 4, 5, 6, etc. Focus on the *one decision* that's right in front of you.

The One Decision Away philosophy is a state of being. It's how you show up in the world each day and how you live your life. You can live by default and just go through the motions, or you can live by design and focus on making *one decision* each day. Keep it simple.

I never worry about what I need to do in the future. I am aware of it, but instead, I focus on being better today than I was yesterday. That happens by acting on the *one decision* that I need to make that's in front of me each day. Unfortunately, most people live in the gap of hesitation. They know they are only *one decision away* from what they need to do, but instead, they make excuses and give themselves all the reasons not to do something. Is this how you truly want to live? Accepting your life for what it is instead of leading yourself to where you want to go? Let me remind you. You have breath. You have fresh air. You have a heartbeat. You still have time. Your life isn't over. It doesn't matter how old you are. Stop letting the life you were meant to live slip away from you! Your better future is just *one decision away.*

The One Decision Away philosophy isn't just a mindset – it's backed by science to propel you toward success. And this is what excites me the most! Think about a Saturday when you have a list of errands to run. As you check off each task, you feel a surge of satisfaction, right? That's not just in your head. There's a reason for it.

Author and motivational speaker Tony Robbins says the #1 source of fulfillment is progress. I agree with this statement. Every time you complete a task, no matter how small, you feel a sense of accomplishment. But here's where it gets even more powerful. This feeling isn't just psychological; it's biological. Your brain's ventral tegmental area releases dopamine, the neurotransmitter responsible for motivation, movement, and reward.

So, when you focus on just one decision – the next most important step – you trigger that dopamine release, fueling your momentum to keep going. Success isn't about over-whelming yourself with everything at once; it's about making *one decision* at a time and letting your brain's chemistry work in your favor. Boom! This is why I believe in the One Decision Away philosophy so much. Because it's not just a philosophy – it's a science-backed strategy for unstoppable progress.

Want to know my biggest fear? Want to know what drives me? Want to know how I stay in that mental state and focus on always being *one decision away?* I fear living with regret. That scares me. The thought of looking back and saying to myself, "I wish I had done this." or "I wish I did that." That will keep me up at night. That scares me. Maybe it's because I am 47 now, and life to me, more than ever, seems to be flying by. Both my in-laws are no longer with us. My Dad was diagnosed with Alzheimer's disease this past year, and seeing his changes scares me. People around my age have passed away from sudden illnesses. It's eye-opening. Just last month, some plaque was found on one of the main arteries of my heart, and my doctor told me, "You can't outrun genetics." It scared me. High blood pressure and high cholesterol run in my family, so even though I exercise daily and eat healthy (most of the time), I now have this to deal with. I cannot waste any time, and neither should you. I have big goals. I have dreams. I have a vision for my life to make a huge impact on the world and give my family an amazing life. But now I realize I am the next generation after my parents, so I cannot waste time. We all get 24 hours each day. Once it's over, there is no turning back. The clock is always ticking. So, I always ask myself, "What is the *one decision* I need to make today to move my life forward?" It's a simple way for me to win the day. Will some of the decisions I need to make be difficult? Of course. There are no perfect decisions. But the key is to make them *one decision* at a time.

I want to remind you of something as you navigate your life and start to focus on the *one decision* you need to make today to move your life forward. You need to make decisions based on principles, not your emotions. I will have an entire chapter about this later in the book, but let me briefly cover it here. The Oxford Language Dictionary defines principles as "fundamental truths." For example, you may not feel like exercising today (an emotion), but you know that you are a healthier human today for it by doing the workout (life's principle of exercise). Another example is that you may not feel like putting up that business social media post (i.e., emotions of feeling tired, fear of what others may think, etc.), but by doing it anyway, you know it can positively impact your business (principle). Our emotions promise us nothing in the end. But principles are tried and true.

In the next chapter, I will share with you how the rest of this book will be broken down so you can apply the One Decision Away philosophy to your life. But for now, I need you to acknowledge that this is a straightforward philosophy to understand, but we, as human beings, always overcomplicate things. I can guarantee you that right now, as you read this, there is *one decision* you could make today that could alter your life's path for the better.

FOCUS ON THE ONE DECISION YOU NEED TO MAKE TODAY.

It doesn't need to be some big, grandiose decision. It's often the tiny little decisions we make each day, usually barely noticeable, that compounded over time lead to massive success. So don't be looking for some massive, big life-or-death decision you need to make today. It's the simple, probably slightly uncomfortable decision you know in your gut you need to make. Furthermore, don't worry about what you will do after that. Life will reveal that to you in due time. Focus on the *one decision* you need to make today.

3 Key Takeaways

1. Face Your Fears with Courage

Fear often prevents people from taking action, whether it's fear of failure, success, or judgment. Recognize that fear is natural but not life-threatening in most situations. Instead of waiting to "feel ready," take courageous action despite fear. Remember, every fear you've faced so far, you've overcome — you're still here. Courage is the first step to making decisions that move you forward.

2. Embrace Faith in the Unknown

Making decisions often requires faith — the belief in things you cannot yet see. While obstacles are inevitable, having faith that you'll learn and grow through challenges helps you stay committed to your goals. Trust that life will reveal the next steps after you make the decision in front of you. Focus on progress, not perfection, and let faith guide you through uncertainty.

3. Principles over Emotions

Base your decisions on fundamental truths (principles) rather than fleeting emotions. For example, even if you don't feel like exercising, do it because the principle of health matters. Principles provide consistent, long-term benefits, while emotions can lead to inaction or regret. By aligning your daily decisions with principles, you set yourself up for sustainable growth and success. I will get into more detail in this later in the book.

CHAPTER 2

How to Apply the One Decision Away Philosophy

ow that I have explained how the One Decision Away philosophy came to be – even though it's been a way of life my whole life – and defined it for you, I want to go over how the rest of this book will be laid out. It will almost be like a guide that you can use to reflect on your past life and plan ahead to apply this philosophy in the future.

After I had the realization both in my hotel room and while speaking on stage, I needed some time to think more about the philosophy. To take a deep dive into this state of being. I knew at this point that my second book was in the making, so I took a piece of paper out and wrote in big letters "ONE DECISION AWAY" in the middle of it and then brain dumped everything I thought about it. I wrote everything down in no specific order and put circles around each main thought.

These became the chapters of this book. I then took a step back, looked at everything I wrote, and recognized three distinct parts.

The first part has to do with some of my research that proves that many of the *decisions* I made in my own life or others have made, which may have seemed so small at the time, massively transformed our lives. Additionally, as I was looking at everything I wrote down, I noticed one repeating thought that is important to mention before we go any further. This is regret and how your decisions, or lack thereof, can impact you or others.

The second part of the book is another underlying theme I noticed during my brainstorming session, which was all the obstacles that commonly get in our way as we focus each day on making the *one decision*. Nothing in life worth fighting for will ever come easy. Every single day, the *one decision* you need to make to move your life forward is not going to be like the decision of whether or not to brush your teeth. Sorry, I wish it was that easy. Rather, it's the *one decision* you know you need to make that will make you feel slightly uncomfortable, but you know in your heart and gut it's the right one. We will all face common obstacles and ultimately will need to overcome them to be successful. I think it's important to talk to you about these obstacles, so you don't feel alone, you understand what you are going through, and that what you are feeling is normal. Most importantly, understanding that obstacles are part of the growth process for your life, and you need to go through them. Or, as I like to say, "grow" through them. So, the second part of the book is all the expected obstacles you will face.

The third part of this book will teach you how to apply the One Decision Away philosophy to your life. In essence, the *one decision away* state of being incorporates a tool in your thought process to face these obstacles along the way. But I will give you multiple tools (throughout different chapters) to use so that when you face life's challenges and make that *one decision,* you are mentally prepared to overcome it.

It's kind of a mindset dance that will be with you throughout your life. It never goes away. No matter where you are in your life, there will always be room to grow and expand your potential. So if you wake up each day and focus on the one thing you need to do today to be better than you were yesterday, aka the one decision, you can expect that right around the corner, an obstacle will be in your way. You then need the mindset tool to overcome the obstacle to move forward in your life. Each day, your mindset will dance back and forth between the decision you need to make and the obstacle that will try to prevent you from acting. Make sense? Don't over-complicate it. Ultimately, we are always only one decision away from changing our lives. It's that simple.

Before we move on to the next chapter, I want you to understand that you don't eventually master the mindset tools I will share with you

IT'S A MINDSET DANCE THAT WILL BE WITH YOU THROUGHOUT YOUR LIFE.

and then life's decisions become easy. Life will never be easy, and there will always be a decision you make today that could improve your life. The hard decisions often bring us the most value in our lives. We will always face obstacles along the way. We may be better prepared to handle them because we have developed mindset callouses from the repeated tough decisions we made, but we are human, and our minds are there to protect us. Therefore, this is a work in progress. This book should not be a one-and-done read. I was once told, "David, how about instead of reading a hundred books, you read one book a hundred times." This is a powerful statement. This book should be something you read and refer to often when you feel scared, nervous, lonely, unsure, or worried about what to do next. Or read it more often and stay out in front of an obstacle that may be coming. Why? Because tough times will always occur in our lives and this can be a good reminder of what it takes to stay on track.

Last, I truly believe God wouldn't give you something you cannot handle. The *one decision* you need to make is personal to you and where you are in your life. In the Bible, Matthew 25:21 says, *"Since you were faithful in small matters, I will give you great responsibilities."* In short, we need to learn how to make the *one decision* that is right in front of us before life presents us with an opportunity at a higher level that will require bigger, more challenging decisions. We will only face obstacles at the level of life we are in. When we make these decisions, we grow as human beings and will be prepared for what comes next.

Some may ask if this is a religious book with the two quotes I shared thus far. The short answer is no, but I am a Roman Catholic who actively goes to church with my family, and I am a man of faith. I went to a private Catholic school my entire life; therefore, many of the things I have learned that have positively impacted my life have come from my faith in God. I will unapologetically share it. With that being said, you do not need to be a person of faith or have the same beliefs as me to grow and learn from this book because everyone can learn from what I share and teach here regardless of their religious background.

❸ *Key Takeaways*

1. **Recognize the Power of Small Decisions**

   Even seemingly small decisions can lead to massive transformations in life. Reflecting on past choices helps illustrate how one moment of action, no matter how minor it may seem, can change your trajectory.

2. **Prepare for Obstacles and Embrace Growth**

   Challenges are inevitable when striving for meaningful growth, but these obstacles are part of the process. Adopting the mindset of "growing through" them instead of avoiding them builds resilience.

3. **Adopt a Daily Focus on Progress**

   Making "one decision" each day to improve, even by a small amount, can create momentum. While obstacles may arise, the goal is to cultivate a consistent practice of aligning daily actions with your larger purpose.

PART 1

THE ONE DECISION AWAY PHILOSOPHY: REAL-LIFE PROOF

Whether you realize it or not, the decisions you made, or lack thereof, have brought you to where you are today. You are a product of the decisions you made up until this point. Furthermore, the impact of your decisions doesn't just affect you. It affects everyone around you too. Lastly, no one has ever achieved the highest level of success without making small daily decisions to move forward.

YOU ARE A PRODUCT OF THE DECISIONS YOU MADE UP UNTIL THIS POINT.

CHAPTER 3

The Conversation That Changed My Life

can remember this as if it was yesterday, even though it was about 15 years ago. I would sit in the hallway at a desk in our one-bedroom home for my wife and I to do work. We had an Apple iMac computer on the desk, and looking back, the only time I ever sat there to do any work was to do bills. I wouldn't call this productive work. Sitting there always came with a lot of stress.

My wife Kristen and I were six figures in debt between credit cards, student loans, car payments, and more. We didn't make the wisest choices early on during our marriage. Even though I was an investigator with the state police making six figures and Kristen was a schoolteacher with her master's degree, also making good money, we struggled. They say when you make more, you tend to spend more. That was us. The debt just grew, and I routinely would open new zero-interest credit cards for a certain number of months and transfer debt from one credit card to the other to avoid paying interest. It was a horrible way to live. But this wasn't the worst part. The worst part was the arguing we would have over money. I remember constantly arguing over things such as the grocery bill.

Twice a month, I would sit down to pay the bills, and I knew before I even sat down that I would end up in a bad mood, very stressed out, and often arguing with my wife. To make matters worse, we both weren't in the best of shape. I was about 25 lbs. overweight, and Kristen struggled to lose the baby weight from having our daughters. So, we were frequently tired, had minimal energy, felt run down, and clearly did not handle stress very well. We were surviving, not thriving.

I remember the mental games I would play with myself. I would get new credit cards with zero interest, transfer our debt, work as much overtime as possible to try to get ahead, and then wait for our next contract so I would get a pay raise. The truth was this all happened. I would make more, get a new contract, and get new credit cards, but nothing changed. I finally realized that I needed to take complete ownership of my life. I could no longer wait for someone or something to rescue me. My success depended on me.

Around the same time this happened, my close friend finally got me to try P90X, a Beachbody at home workout program, after months of him pressuring me to try it. I was very against this at-home style workout, but I had nothing to lose at this point, so I went all in. I got unbelievable results in the 90 days of the program, and I remember seeing a business opportunity with Beachbody. It seemed pretty simple. You share your success story with others; if they are interested, they can purchase the program through you.

You then guide and help them along in their journey. I became a walking billboard with my results and even started earning extra income. But what intrigued me more was seeing other people earning substantial income doing the same thing. So I asked myself, "Could this be the very thing that can get me healthy and fit while also getting me out of this financial stress?" As weeks went on, my vision grew, and I started seeing myself growing this business. Kristen noticed what I was doing but didn't say much. She watched from afar. However, eventually, she started giving me a hard time for being on my phone all the time because I was always preoccupied. I wasn't "present" during dinner, and often, when we were talking or with our kids, I was on the phone. It was a mental tug-of-war between chasing the vision to earn extra income to pay our debt off, which would decrease our stress, or being present with my family. I knew something needed to give.

I remember how nervous I was when I realized I needed to have a serious talk with Kristen. I truly believed in my vision of what this business could do for us. I had that butterfly feeling in my gut and knew it was a sign I needed to pursue. It was the same butterfly feeling I had when I knew I needed to read that book about keynote speaking shared in the introduction. I felt that fire in my belly and had that gut feeling. For my entire life up until this point, whenever I set my mind to do something, I did whatever it took to make it happen. This was no different. I was hesitant and nervous about talking to Kristen about my vision. I wanted her support and to possibly ask her to join me on this journey. But I feared she would be against it or dismiss the idea. That she would not want to support me because I needed to be more present with my family. Some of her concerns would be absolutely right. The inner dialogue I was having was off the charts, but I couldn't sit still any longer.

When your desire for change is stronger than your desire to stay the same, you will find a way. Otherwise, you will find an excuse. At this point, I knew I was done with living the way we were living and that something needed to change. It was time. So, I asked to speak to her when we were alone. Not in passing when the kids were running around the kitchen during dinnertime, but in a conversation with just her and me.

That night, after the kids went to bed, we sat down at our kitchen table, and as nervous and hesitant as I was, I looked her straight in the eye and said, "Babe, I truly believe this Beachbody business can change our life. I am sorry I haven't been present. You are right. But we cannot continue anymore the way we are. In debt, living paycheck to paycheck. It's way too much stress. I am asking you for your support and to help me find a way to work this business while still being present with the family."

WHEN YOUR DESIRE FOR CHANGE IS STRONGER THAN YOUR DESIRE TO STAY THE SAME, YOU WILL FIND A WAY.

Kristen still says today that she wanted to believe my vision at the time, but she didn't. I don't blame her. The negativity surrounding multi-level marketing (which Beachbody was) was everywhere. She also thought, "people like us don't achieve big things like that in our lives." But she wanted to support me.

Kristen agreed to let me work on the business, but we agreed on work hours for when I could and could not work. I would only work after the kids went to bed, which I did every single night from 8 p.m. to 11 p.m. I sacrificed sleep, watching television, playing in softball leagues, and a handful of other social things to work my business instead.

This went on for years, and to my surprise, Kristen both started doing the workouts with me (and got in great shape, I must say! Baby weight bye-bye!), but she also started working the business as well! This is another story, but here is the part I want to share next.

Beachbody had quarterly events called Super Saturdays. They were local events put on by coaches to network, meet coaches in your area, and hear about the latest company news. Coaches who had some success were asked to speak and share their stories during the event. This one Saturday, when I was helping organize the event at the local library, I was asked to speak and share my success story of building the business while married with three kids, my struggles, how I overcame them, and so on. I agreed to do it, and it was in front of about 15 people. I think 17 was the exact number, but it was over 12 years ago, so I may be wrong.

I went up to speak and share my story; to my surprise, it came naturally to me. I didn't stand behind the podium. I didn't use note cards to refer to. I went off memory and gave a 15-minute motivational talk. I finished and said, "I can't wait to do this again!" It should be noted that the fear of public speaking is the most common phobia ahead of death, spiders, or heights. The National Institute of Mental Health reports that public speaking anxiety affects about 73% of the population.

A few months later, I was asked to speak again, this time to a larger group of about 50 people. Then I was asked again, and it grew to about 100 people. Then 250 people. Then a 1000. Then, ultimately, I found myself speaking to 20,000 people in the NFL Super Dome on stage at Beachbody's annual premier event, sharing my story. This day I will never forget. I had a profound emotional moment that day. After walking off stage and finding my way back to the audience to sit down next to Kristen, I glanced at my phone, and it was blowing up with text messages. "David, that was hands down the best coach story I have ever heard." "Dude, you are a natural on stage!" "David, you brought me to tears. Your story was beyond powerful." I immediately got overwhelmed by the flood of messages on my phone and cried. I was overwhelmed with all the emotions. Joy, happiness, sadness (onstage I shared the story of losing my best friend, which I share in my first book, *The Leveled Up Life*), and more simultaneously. Kristen didn't know what was happening until I asked her for tissues and showed her the text messages. It was an extremely emotional moment for me because the feeling I just had walking off stage was exhilarating, followed by all the messages I was getting from so many people about my presentation, which pushed me over the top. Hence, I cried.

Furthermore, you know that feeling you get after a great workout? You feel so good you think you can run through a brick wall? Your emotions are running so high in a positive way that you want to bottle it up? Well, that's how I feel when I get off stage after I speak. Typical for me but not normal for others.

After I got up from my seat, one final distinct memory happened that day. I went to use the restroom and ran into one of the executives of Beachbody. He couldn't say enough about my story on stage and said something to me at the end of our conversation I will never forget. He said, "David, you should be a speaker. You are a natural on stage." Whoa! What?! Between feeling like I was on cloud nine walking off the stage, to the tears I had from reading all my texts, and now this? Is this a sign? Is this my next one decision to make, presented right in front of me? Well, it sure seemed like it because that butterfly feeling of pursuing becoming a speaker was born that very day.

When I speak on stage, I often say, "God's gift to us is potential. Our gift back is what we do with it." Speaking and pouring into others was a gift I never knew I had. It was never something I had planned on in my life or pursued. Life presented it to me. I always thought I would be a New York State Trooper for 30-plus years and then retire with my pension to live happily ever after. But not anymore. God had other plans. Here, I was full of emotions, seeing a completely different future in my path.

I could share with you the next decision I made to retire from the state police at 43 years old to pursue being a speaker because that, too, was just as scary with all the self-doubt, fear, emotions, and lack of support. But rather than doing that, I want to share something even more important and influential. As I sit here today writing my second book with a podcast and now traveling all around the country speaking to thousands of people for all sorts of industries, none of this would have ever happened if it wasn't for the one decision I made to have a conversation with Kristen that night. That conversation led to a successful business that got us healthy, financially out of debt, and opened the door to a gift I never knew I had as a speaker. Then, once I decided to retire to become a speaker, I made the one decision to write a book. Then one decision to start a podcast. Now I sit here writing a second book after this one decision. How did this all happen? It's because of the one decision I made to push through all the negative emotions and fear I had to talk to my wife. It was that one decision. The *one decision* you need to make today is different for everybody. It may be a business idea, a healthier lifestyle, a conversation with your significant other, and so on. Only you know what that is, but we all have something in our life that we need to make that one decision on.

Like I have said before we must stop worrying about how we will achieve that big goal ten steps ahead and instead focus on the *one decision* to be better today. The rest will reveal itself for you as it has for me. What is the *one decision* that can improve your life today? It's that simple. *One decision* will lead to the next *one decision*, and that *one decision*

YOUR ANSWER IS RIGHT IN FRONT OF YOU. #ONEDECISIONAWAY

will lead you to the next one. We must keep it simple. Your answer is right in front of you. #OneDecisionAway

❸ Key Takeaways

1. Take Responsibility for Your Future

Waiting for circumstances or others to change your situation only keeps you stuck. Progress begins when you take full responsibility for your health, finances, and career. The first step toward change is recognizing that no one is coming to save you – it's on you to create the life you want. What area of your life do you need to take ownership of today?

2. Courageous Conversations Can Unlock Transformation

The pivotal moment in my journey came when I faced my fears and had an honest conversation with my wife, Kristen. That one discussion created a new level of understanding and set the stage for everything that followed – financial freedom, personal growth, and even my speaking career. If there's a conversation you've been avoiding, it might just be the key to unlocking your next breakthrough.

3. Focus on the Next Step, Not the Whole Journey

Instead of worrying about the ten steps ahead, focus on the one decision in front of you. Each small step, like committing to P90X, sharing my story, or staying disciplined with work hours, created momentum and led to unexpected opportunities. Don't let the big picture overwhelm you – ask yourself: what's one decision you can make today to improve your life? Trust that each step will reveal the next.

CHAPTER 4

Who Else Applied the One Decision Away Philosophy (and maybe didn't even know it)?

s I began thinking more and more about this book and started doing some of my own research, I couldn't believe the number of success stories I came across about celebrities that applied the One Decision Away philosophy to their own life, especially early on when they weren't famous. Not only have I recognized that this philosophy applied to my whole life, but the more I studied successful people, the more I came across very powerful one decision away life stories.

Before I share some of these stories with you, I noticed an underlying theme in all these successful people you need to know. Not only did they all focus on moving forward on the decisions they needed to make that day, but they all had a bigger VISION for their life. They all saw themselves achieving something much more extraordinary in their life than where they were at that present moment. They had goals. They had dreams. They had a vision, and they were relentless in their pursuit of making that dream a reality. They never quit. They demonstrated perseverance and grit during times when the average person would quit and give up. Their vision was so big and clear in their minds that nothing would stop them from achieving it.

This makes me think of a few questions you need to ask yourself. What are your goals and dreams today? What price are you willing to pay to make those dreams become a reality? With absolute certainty, the greats of all time always made up their mind first that they would achieve success no matter what. Nothing was going to stop them. They didn't have a Plan B in their brain because having a Plan B in their mindset before they even started immediately gave them a way out. They would see it as settling. Your vision has to be so powerful that when you shut your eyes, you can see yourself achieve it before you are even there! You can taste it, see it, and smell it. Not literally, but I think you know what I mean. It must be that powerful. There is no questioning it.

YOUR VISION HAS TO BE SO POWERFUL THAT WHEN YOU SHUT YOUR EYES, YOU CAN SEE YOURSELF ACHIEVE IT BEFORE YOU ARE EVEN THERE.

Too many people are not pursuing their dreams because they let "life" stop them. When I speak, I often do a live poll with the audience. I first ask them, "For everyone who has dreams for their life, please raise your hand." I then say, "Keep your hands up if you are actively pursuing your dreams." About 1/2 or more of the hands go down. Then I finally say, "Keep your hands up if you actually achieved your dreams." Most times, in a room of about 300-500 people, I may get 1-2 people who still have their hands up. Sometimes none. That means, on average, more than 99 percent of people in the room haven't achieved their dreams. Think about that. We accept our life for what it is rather than leading it to where we want it to go. At some point, we may suffer from regret. I am sure this may apply to you if I ask you the same questions. But remember, if you are reading this book, that means you have a heartbeat, you have breath, you have fresh air, and you still have time in your life. It's never too late. Your next step is truly just *one decision away*.

Michael Jordan, arguably the best basketball player of all time with a net worth of over 3 billion dollars, was cut from his varsity basketball team, which could have easily crushed his spirit. He said, "I can accept failure. Everyone fails at something. But I can't accept not trying." He instead had to play on the junior varsity team, where he worked on his skills and developed a work ethic like no other. Rather than give up or worry about the following year's tryouts, he focused on what he needed to do in the moments following his setback after getting cut from varsity. He made the *one decision* that he was going to press forward, continue to work on his development, and strive to be the best he could be no matter what. The vision he had for his life and the choice he made to take action on the *one decision* that was right in front of him brought him to where he is today. The G.O.A.T. of basketball with six NBA Championships and arguably one of the best athletes of all time. He is the epitome of the One Decision Away philosophy.

Do you know who was richer than Queen Elizabeth II of England? J.K. Rowling, the famous author of *Harry Potter* now has a net worth of over 1 billion dollars. On her website, she recalls,

> In 1990, after moving to London, I was sitting on a delayed train back home from Manchester when suddenly I had the idea of a boy wizard who went to wizarding school. Harry Potter and Hogwarts came out of nowhere in the most physical rush of excitement, and ideas came teeming into my head. I simply knew it was something I would love to write, but that day, I was pen-less for once in my life, so as I sat there on the train, I had to rely on imagining the details, most of which ended up being in the books. From the start, I knew there would be seven books, and I had the whole story plotted out early on. It took me five years to write the first book in the series.

J.K. Rowling was a single mother who struggled to make ends meet while living in an Edinburgh apartment that was infested with rats. In Edinburgh, she trained as a teacher and began teaching in the city's schools, but she continued to write in every spare moment. Between having a baby and a typewriter, she would go to the local cafe anytime she could to write. After the 5 years it took her to write her first book, 12 different publishers denied it until finally it was accepted by Christopher Little, an obscure London literary agent. The rest is history. I don't even know where to start when it comes to her story. There is so much to unpack, but multiple times throughout her journey, she always made the *one decision* that was right in front of her. First, it was the *one decision* to write and follow her gut with this exciting idea that was teeming into her head. Then, the vision she had for all seven books and the series of *one decisions* she had to make to keep writing at any spare moment for well over 5 years! That's unbelievable consistency! Then, the decision she made, no matter how many times she was rejected, to keep sending her manuscript to more publishers. She just kept focusing on the *one decision* she needed to make each day that was in front of her, paired with relentless perseverance until she finally got a yes! Her vision finally became a reality. I love everything about her story because it is a testament to how the *one decision away* philosophy truly works. Your vision appears. You follow your gut. You keep showing up each day and putting in the work. You don't worry about what to do tomorrow. You focus on the *one decision* you need to make today by keeping your vision at the forefront and never giving up until you succeed. When you focus on taking action on the *one decision* in front of you, the rest will take care of itself. One day at a time. This is beyond powerful on so many levels and should remind us all of what it may truly take to be successful. However, to get there, it is always only *one decision away*.

This next person I want to talk about truly manifested his dreams and is a true testament to the power of visualization. He is one of the most famous actors in the world, with a net worth of 180 million dollars. That person is Jim Carrey. At 12 years old, Jim's father lost his job, which was the family's only source of income. They couldn't afford a place to live, so at 16 years old, Jim dropped out of school to go to work and help support his family. Jim worked as a janitor but always had a passion for comedy and acting, so he did everything he could to pursue that. He struggled to make a name for himself in Hollywood but always visualized being one of the top actors in the world. He would picture himself super busy with all the directors who wanted to work with him. He recalls a specific point in time when he wrote a check out to himself for 10 million dollars and postdated it 10 years later on Thanksgiving Day 1995 for "acting services rendered." Well, guess what? Ten years later, he was cast in the famous movie *Dumb and Dumber*, and for how much? You guessed it: 10 million dollars. Incredible! He had a vision for his future, often closing his eyes and visualizing himself already achieving it. Since he felt so strongly about it, he posted a check to himself for 10 million dollars. Without question, every single day, he followed his gut and made the *one decision* each day to keep showing up and pursuing his dream. He was relentless in staying committed day in and day out, taking the necessary actions that day to pursue it. Having that vision was *one decision* he made. Writing that check was another *one decision* he made. Showing up every day were consistent *one decisions* he made. He truly lived the One Decision Away philosophy.

The last story I want to share with you is from someone who once said, "All our dreams can come true if we have the courage to pursue them." Since his passing, the company today is worth 164 billion dollars. This person is Walt Disney. His story is full of perseverance, self-belief, visualization, and an unbelievable imagination. Walt Disney was always very interested in the arts from a very young age. At 4 years old, he drew a portrait of his neighbor's house, and from 9-15 years old, he worked part-time delivering newspapers while taking courses in cartooning. When he got a little bit older, he moved to Hollywood to pursue his dream but faced a lot of rejection. After a string of rejections day in and day out, he and his brother decided to open the Walt Disney Company to produce films since he had no luck working with anyone else. Soon thereafter, the Disney company found success in its creation of the famous Mickey Mouse and thus produced two cartoon series. He then made the renowned movie *Snow White and the Seven Dwarfs*, which was massively successful. From there, he produced *Pinocchio, Fantasia, Dumbo*, and *Bambi* in the 1940s with even more success. This led to his dream of building multiple amusement parks, which started with Disneyland in California. Many didn't believe he could do it, and he often had a hard time obtaining funds for the parks. However, he kept his vision alive, spending 5 more years developing his ideas, which were sometimes called the "impossible dream." Walt Disney went on to win 22 Academy Awards and passed away in 1966 at 65 years old, but his company is still a massive success. How? He dreamed big, following his vision every single day by making the next *decision* that was in front of him to move his dreams forward. Even in the face of adversity, he persevered, and the more success he had, the bigger he dreamed, continuously taking action on the next *decision*. He made a profound impact on the world today and will continue to leave an impact and legacy for many generations to come.

I can't stress enough the power of the One Decision Away philosophy. It doesn't matter where you are in your life right now. You can use this mindset tool to recognize at any moment, you are always only *one decision away* from a different life. We too often beat ourselves up because of our past, which we can't change, or we worry too much about our future, which we have no control over. Let all of that go! It doesn't matter. What matters is what you decide to do today at this very moment. To take action or not. Let me share a few testimonials from people in the audience at some of my recent keynotes to give you some more perspective:

"We all have a purpose in life and David motivated me today to realize to never give up. I am about to turn 70 years old, and I was just about ready to give up. His speech and message today inspired me in such a way that we're never too old, and we should never give up on things that God has placed in our hearts and in our minds."

"I can't tell you what an impact the kick-off with David Atkins has made on my life. The good Lord works in mysterious ways – ONE DECISION AWAY!"

"It was truly emotional, and it was motivating, but I think the biggest thing for me, and I think my wife expressed it too, was that it's one decision, and for me, as I'm getting older, that it's never too late and just do it. Go for it, and don't give up."

There are many testimonials I can share, but the common theme above is that you are never too old, don't ever give up, and you are always only *one decision away*. It is time you believe in yourself in this very moment and understand that whatever dreams or goals you have in your heart and mind, you can achieve them. Between the celebrity stories I shared above, my own story, or even these recent testimonials shared, it's not just possible – It's past possible! It's *one decision away*.

❸ Key Takeaways

1. **Dream Big and Create a Clear Vision**

   Every successful person featured in this chapter
   – whether it's Michael Jordan, J.K. Rowling, Jim
   Carrey, or Walt Disney – had an unwavering vision
   for their future. They could see their goals so vividly in their mind that it drove them forward, even
   when faced with setbacks and rejection. Take time
   today to reflect on your own dreams and visualize
   your success. If you can see it clearly, you're one
   step closer to making it a reality.

2. **Focus on the One Decision You Can Make Right Now**

   These stories remind us that success isn't about
   doing everything at once; it's about doing the next
   right thing. Michael Jordan didn't dwell on getting
   cut from varsity; he worked on his game. J.K. Rowling
   kept writing one chapter at a time. The same applies
   to you – don't let the big picture overwhelm you.
   Ask yourself, "What one decision can I make today
   to move closer to my goal?"

3. **Persevere and Never Give Up**

   Setbacks, failures, and rejection are inevitable on
   the path to success, but perseverance is what separates dreamers from achievers. Jim Carrey struggled to make ends meet, J.K. Rowling faced years of
   rejection, and Walt Disney was told his dreams were
   impossible. Yet, they kept going. Remember, every
   obstacle is temporary, but your commitment to your

vision must be permanent. Don't quit – you're always *one decision away* from the breakthrough you've been waiting for.

CHAPTER 5

What if You Weren't Willing to Try?

The fear of looking back on my life and saying, "I wish I did this" or "I wish I did that," scares me. So much so that, at times, this is one of my driving forces to strive to be my best. I don't want to live with regret. I've never felt more strongly about this than I do now. Maybe it's because I see what's happening all around me these last few years as I enter my later 40's. Friends are losing their parents; my wife lost both of her parents, and then what scares me the most are a few parents around the same age as me who I have known, that suddenly passed away from something such as a heart attack or an illness that they struggled with. I want to think we have all the time in the world, but we don't. Time is something we can never get back. We can never slow down the clock. I do my very best to slow the aging process, such as being an active and healthy adult to prolong my life, but this doesn't remove the fear of regret. It just hopefully buys me more time.

I am married with three teenage daughters, and the last thing I would want to face many years from now is looking at the three of them and saying, "Girls, your dad had all this potential to do amazing things for our family, but it got too hard, and I let fear get the best of me. I'm sorry. I wish I could have done better." That haunts me, and it should for you, too. For all the parents out there, it should motivate you to be your very best each day and stop making excuses for your life.

I once read that you can pay now and play later, or you can play now and pay later. Either way, you will need to pay. What does this mean? You can either pay the price now by working hard to be your very best so that later on in life, you can reap the rewards and play, or you can waste away and play with your life now, but later on, you will pay the price, such as regret. You decide. It's a choice.

YOU CAN PAY NOW AND PLAY LATER, OR YOU CAN PLAY NOW AND PAY LATER.

I was having a conversation with someone about a week ago about a goal and dream they had for something in their life. But as they were talking, they listed all the reasons why it may not work and the potential obstacles they may face along the way. My first question back to this person was:

"What if it didn't turn out that way?"

"What if you actually did do it and all the obstacles you just listed didn't happen."

"What do you lose by at least trying? Nothing. You have nothing to lose."

"But if you aren't willing to at least try, you guarantee one thing. Failure."

I then followed up, saying, "Why not you?! Why can't you be the guy to have good things happen?! Stop looking at what could go wrong with it and start looking at what could go right with it!"

Far too many people sell themselves short. You must be willing to try. If it's that important, you must at least take a chance. You have nothing to lose by trying and everything to gain. But by not trying, you have everything to lose. People like this are deep in negative thinking, and the more they think about potential problems, the bigger they become. It's like a weed that starts growing out of control in your brain. If you are reading this and can think of something you wanted to pursue in the past but found yourself listing all the reasons why it won't work, I want you to remember this. First, you must be willing to try so you don't regret it later. Second, you are *one decision away* from taking action on your first step, right now, today.

I'll never forget the story that author and owner of Vayner-Media Gary Vaynerchuk shared about interviewing people at a nursing home about their life and, looking back, they offered one piece of advice for the younger generation. It often started with "I wish I did this, or I wish I did that." They had regrets. They say the wealthiest place on earth is the graveyard because it's full of goals, dreams, and ideas that were never acted upon. Don't become part of this reality!

If you have regrets in your life up until now, I want you to give yourself some grace. It's okay. Far too many people beat themselves up for decisions they made in the past. You will come out of this, and here are a few tips to help you cope with regret.

First, accept who you are and understand that your value in life is not based on your mistakes. Practice some self-compassion and stop beating yourself up because we are all constantly learning and growing as we navigate life. As mentioned above, give yourself some grace. You are human. No one is perfect. We all make mistakes and have regrets at some point in life. So, accept what happened, learn from it, and immediately focus on improving by making the *one decision* to move forward.

Second, if you feel that a bad decision you made has affected other people, consider apologizing to them. Not only would they likely appreciate it, but subconsciously, you will feel good by apologizing to that person. You also are taking ownership of your mistakes and not giving power to someone else over your life, and apologizing releases that because you take back feeling in control. You own it and can move forward.

Lastly, you need to take action right away in your new direction. You need to make the *one decision* today on whatever that means to you to press forward. No more regrets. No more suffering. You are *one decision away* from a completely different life.

❸ *Key Takeaways*

1. Regret Is the Cost of Inaction

You have nothing to lose by trying and everything to gain. By not taking a chance on your goals or dreams, you guarantee regret. Remember, time is irreplaceable – act now to avoid looking back and wishing you had done more.

2. Shift Your Focus to What Could Go Right

Instead of dwelling on potential obstacles, ask yourself, what if it works? You're *one decision away* from making progress. Choose optimism over fear and take the first step toward your potential.

3. Turn Regret into Growth

If you have regrets, give yourself grace and use those experiences to grow. Accept your mistakes, practice self-compassion, take ownership, and then make the *one decision* to move forward. Your best life starts now – leave regret behind.

CHAPTER 6

It Affects More
Than Just You

clearly remember a time where my wife and I were standing outside our youngest daughter's bedroom. The bedroom door was shut, and we overheard our 16-year-old daughter giving our 9-year-old a pep talk. At the time, our 9-year-old struggled with self-confidence, so our oldest daughter decided to be a good big sister and tried to help her out. My wife and I were so blown away by the things that she was saying that I took my phone out and recorded the conversation. It's as if all the things we have been preaching to our daughters for years, which they often made fun of us for or told us we don't understand, were actually working because our oldest daughter was saying the exact same things to our youngest. I went back and listened to the conversation, and I want to share some of it with you.

"Love yourself for who you are today."

"You won't stay this way forever."

"Your body will change and won't stay that way forever, so learn to love yourself now."

"You will change but not right away, so learn to love yourself while you will keep growing."

"Your height doesn't matter, and most boys love girls who are shorter anyway."

"Don't compare yourself to anyone, even your friends or your other sister."

"Be happy for your friends."

"If your friends say something negative, tell them 'no' and don't let them."

"I've seen some of your TikTok's and people say, 'you are so pretty.'"

"Take the little compliments you get."

My oldest then finished her pep talk and offered up a movie they could go watch together.

My wife and I were literally in tears when we heard all this. For one, our oldest was such a great role model and big sister. Hearing the things she said was beyond touching and emotional. But second was the fact that everything we have been teaching them for so long may have actually sunk in. It was a full circle moment for us as we were seeing what we said being passed down.

But here's the more significant thing that my wife and I spoke about after. Little did we know then when we decided to make the one decision to improve our lives for the better by both exercising and reading personal development books that it would affect our kids and potentially future grand-kids in such a way. Everything we read about and learned we would often share with our three daughters, but more importantly, we also practiced what we preached. This was even more important. Why? Because we think our kids only learn from what we say when, in reality, they watch every single thing we do. How we handle adversity. How we show up each day. The energy we bring into the household. How we treat others. The family values we instill. We are far from perfect, but everything we learned about from making the one decision to start improving our own life is now impacting them and potentially the generations of our family that come after us.

Still, today, when my daughters are struggling with anything in life, I always try to give them perspective and what they can learn from it. I will admit, more times than not, they often roll their eyes and say something like, "Dad, I don't need one of your motivational speeches again. You just don't understand." Ha! This comes with the territory of raising teenagers (which some of you may relate to), but clearly, what happened with my oldest and youngest daughter is an example that it is working. They may not want to hear what we have to say, but they, indeed, are listening.

It is very easy to only think of ourselves when we decide on whether to make the *one decision* to improve our life, but in reality, what we do or don't do affects everyone around us. Not only our families but our co-workers, our friends, our extended family. The ripple effect we can have on others by what we do or don't do is much more powerful than you think.

Remember, at the end of the day, people will not remember the cars that you drove or the house that you lived in, but everyone will remember how you made them feel. The impact you can make on others by the decisions you make each day far outweighs anything else. We cannot take our material possessions to the graveyard with us. What we own dies when we do. But the impact we can make on others based on our decisions can carry on for a lifetime.

AT THE END OF THE DAY, PEOPLE WILL NOT REMEMBER THE CARS THAT YOU DROVE OR THE HOUSE THAT YOU LIVED IN, BUT EVERYONE WILL REMEMBER HOW YOU MADE THEM FEEL.

I want to share a story with you that proved to me over and over that the impact you have on others and the feelings that come along with it far outweigh any money you can earn or "things" you can buy. Often, after I finish my keynote presentations, I have a book signing with my first book, *The Leveled Up Life*, for people in the audience. It allows me to interact and meet some special hard-working people. I often get to hear their stories and how my message may have impacted their life. This one story will stick with me forever. I had just finished my keynote and was talking to a person who had just received a signed copy of my book. A few people back, I saw this lady with tears in her eyes as she stood in line to see me. She was visibly upset and nervous as she waited. I naturally became a little anxious to talk to her. When she finally got to the front of the line with tears in her eyes, she trembled, telling me how much she needed to hear my message today. She said, "David, I feel like God came through your lips to my ears. I needed to hear this today." This gave me chills. This lady shared with me how much she was going through. She said she was meant to hear my message today. I got teary-eyed talking to her, and she gave me a big hug as we ended our conversation.

At a separate event, a person in the audience came up and said, "I am about to turn 70 years old, and I was just about ready to give up." Whoa. I often can't believe some of the things I hear. They are honest, raw, and true emotions. Words are powerful, and hearing things like this makes me very emotional.

After many of my events, when I finally get back to my hotel room and I can sit in a quiet place for a minute and reflect on what just happened, I often find myself overcome by emotions that bring tears to my eyes. I have called my wife at times to tell her how it went and usually get emotional with her on the phone as I share what happened or the things that were said to me. I often then sit in a chair in silence for 10-15 minutes, overcome with emotions. Why? Because there is no feeling like the feelings that come with helping and impacting others positively. Not a new car. Not a new home. Nothing. It's something money can't buy. It's something that comes only with making the *one decision* to serve others with the gifts that were given to you.

I am constantly reminded when this happens that I am exactly where I need to be. I am beyond grateful that I had the courage to face all the fears and criticism that came along with leaning into this path as a motivational speaker, because in spite of it I still made the one decision to pursue it and go all in. If I hadn't made that one decision, then all these people who are struggling in their lives wouldn't have heard my message. To me, not making the one decision to become a speaker would have been selfish. It's not about me. It's about using the gifts God has given every one of us to serve the world. When you do that, you, too, may be overcome with emotions like mine.

What we do with our life is bigger than ourselves, and unfortunately, most people accept their life for what it is rather than lead it to where they want to go. People show up to work with their heads held down, shoulders slumped over, and going through the motions, all while counting the days till the weekend. Is that a way to live? On the other hand, when you make that *one decision* to pursue your dreams, you may never work another day in your life, and come to realize how much of an impact you can make on the world and others. You will feel and experience emotions like you never have before. But you need to start and make the one decision. Again, don't overcomplicate it. You are always only *one decision away* from a completely different life.

🔑 *Key Takeaways*

1. **Your Decisions Create Ripple Effects**

   Every choice you make impacts not just your life but the lives of those around you – your family, friends, coworkers, and even future generations. Lead by example, as your actions will often speak louder than your words.

2. **The Greatest Legacy Is How You Make Others Feel**

   Material possessions fade, but the positive impact you have on others lasts a lifetime. Focus on serving others with the unique gifts you've been given to create a lasting, meaningful legacy.

3. **Pursuing Your Dreams Isn't Selfish — It's Necessary**

   By choosing to lean into your potential, you inspire and uplift others. Whether it's your family watching you grow, or strangers touched by your message, living your purpose empowers others to do the same. Don't hold back – it's bigger than you.

PART 2

OBSTACLES YOU WILL NEED TO OVERCOME

Let's face it. No matter where we are, no matter where we live, and no matter what we do, life will constantly challenge us, throw us curveballs, try to derail us, and constantly remind us that anything worth fighting for will not come easily. You are either in a problem, coming out of a problem, or there is a problem on the horizon tomorrow. So, in the following chapters, I want to share with you some of the most common obstacles that will get in your way when you try to apply the One Decision Away philosophy to improve your life. You need to be reminded you are not alone. We all face tough times, but we are stronger together. So hang in there, and let's dive right in!

> YOU ARE EITHER IN A PROBLEM, COMING OUT OF A PROBLEM, OR THERE IS A PROBLEM ON THE HORIZON TOMORROW.

CHAPTER 7

It Will Be Very Lonely Along the Way

T oo often, we compare our everyday lives to the highlight reels we see on social media. People automatically assume that the people on social media who share the perfect house, with their perfect kids, on their perfect vacation, with their beautiful cars, and their perfect marriage is their reality. It's not. Not even close. They struggle, too. They just aren't willing to share it. In my honest opinion, it would be safe to say that 99 percent of the people you see on social media are unwilling to share their actual reality, struggles, or to be open and honest. Everyone makes their lives out to be perfect. It's nonsense. Even in the simplest of forms when it comes to posting a picture. Everyone has a filter on. Everyone takes 37 of the same pictures until they find the perfect one. It's ridiculous. It's all a facade. It's not reality. But here is the truth: Life is hard, It's very hard. We are either in a problem, coming out of a problem, or there is a problem on the horizon tomorrow. Life is going to knock you down repeatedly, and until you have the mental stamina to push back, it will break you. It's that simple. The mental fortitude it takes to continue making the *one decision* each day to improve your life will not be easy. That's why I believe in pushing ourselves physically, i.e., things like going for a hard run will develop mental grit and perseverance that can carry over to your everyday life.

My main point in this chapter is, truthfully, an important one. You will feel alone at times – a lot. As you strive to become more in your life, grow each day, and make the *one decision* to move forward, you will get lonelier and lonelier along the way. You will start to think and operate differently, which may, by default, distance you from people. I remember how when I made the decision to grow my network marketing business and put my health first, it affected my friendships with my peers. Why? Often, when any of my friends would go out, I would either leave early because I knew I needed to get up early to workout, or I would skip the night out altogether. Sometimes, if everyone ordered lunch or dinner, I wouldn't because I often packed my food since I was trying to pay off debt and stick to my diet. These decisions naturally distanced me from my peers, but I knew what to do to achieve my goals. It was a priority to me. Many of those peers are still some of my best friends, but my point is that when your decisions are not the same as everyone else's, you naturally won't have the same relationship. You may even be excluded from being invited to things because they know what you will say. But that's ok. Setting goals requires sacrifices, and only those who have done it understand.

The same may go for your family or friends. Why? The vast majority of the world live an average life. They go to work Monday-Friday to work their 40-hour-a-week job they often hate. They live paycheck to paycheck and take one family vacation a year if they are lucky. Starting on Monday, they count the days until the weekend. They make a decent income. Nothing extraordinary. They flow through life. Listen, I am not knocking this. If this is you (my guess is it's not, or else you wouldn't be reading this book) and you are happy and content with your life, then kudos to you. Keep doing what you are doing. But if you aren't happy with where you are and decide to make the *one decision* to improve your life, then recognize that you will start to feel isolated along the way because you are committing to a lifestyle that most aren't. You need to be willing to make sacrifices.

You will also need to learn to be your own hero at times. As much as we would love for our family, our friends, and all the people we are connected to on social media to motivate and encourage us daily, that's just not going to happen. You will need to learn how to become your own hero. You will need to be your best cheerleader. No one else is going to do it for you.

What you do in the dark when no one is watching will bring you out into the light. There are countless days and, especially late evenings when I find myself alone in my office working with my family asleep. No one was there to cheer me on. No one was there to motivate me. I had accountability to no one other than myself. This went on for years as I built my business with Beachbody, and I can tell you that I am presently reliving this phase of life as a keynote speaker. I often remind myself that, yes, I have been speaking to large groups of people at Beachbody for over 12 years as a speaker, but as far as being a paid professional speaker, I am only in my third year. It can be very lonely as I wake up each day

ACCEPT THE LONELINESS, AS NOT ONLY SOMETHING YOU NEED TO GO THROUGH, BUT SOMETHING YOU NEED TO GROW THROUGH.

and ask myself, "What is the one decision I need to make today to improve my growth as a speaker?" Then, when I figure out what I need to do, I am by myself 99 percent of the time. It's a lonely journey, but I understand it's all part of the process. You have to be willing to realize that going after a big goal, dream, or vision will be a lonely process. So, when I sit there by myself in my quiet office, I remind myself that all my feelings are entirely normal. You have to be okay with this. It's part of the growing process. I know there are many other driven people like myself who, at this very moment, are feeling the same way. Accept the loneliness, as not only something you need to *go* through, but rather as something you need to *grow* through.

I want to share a story with you I once heard about Dr. James Gills. Dr. Gills is the only person ever to complete six double ironman triathlons, meaning he would complete one full ironman triathlon one day and do another the next day. For those who don't know, a full Ironman triathlon consists of a 2.4-mile swim, a 112-mile bicycle ride, and a marathon (26.2-miles) completed in that order, a total of 140.6 miles. The last one Dr. Gills did, he was 59 years old! Author Jon Gordon asked him, "How did you do it?" Dr. Gills responded, "I have learned to talk to myself instead of listen to myself." If he listened to himself, he would hear all the negative about how there was no way he could finish this race, such as his legs being too tired. Him being too old. It feeling impossible. But if he talked to himself, he could find the words to encourage himself to keep going so he could finish the race. I want you to remember that as you apply the One Decision Away philosophy into your life, you too will experience the loneliness of going after your dreams and big goals and may need to learn to talk to yourself. As I stated above, you need to become your own hero sometimes, and if that means literally talking to yourself out loud (in a whisper, I hope) to keep on going, then so be it. Do just that. Be your best cheerleader and verbally cheer yourself on because it will be lonely at times, but that's quite okay. As you are already learning to apply the One Decision Away philosophy to your life to get started on your goals, remember you can always apply it again to talk to yourself so you never give up.

Loneliness is the first obstacle in this book that I need to share with you because about a year ago before I knew I would write a second book, I found myself emotionally drained talking to my wife about how lonely I feel at times as I try to grow and expand as a speaker. She gave me a little pep talk, agreeing it's part of the process, but more importantly, she said that I needed to share this with people. People need to hear this about feeling lonely. It's something that the 99 percent wouldn't be willing to share. Remember that highlight reel? It's okay to be lonely. It's OK to feel isolated when you make the *one decision* to commit to something. I'm sure many people quit when they feel this. They blame other people, play the victim, or blame their circumstances for why it didn't work when, in reality, they are going through the growing pains of being lonely as they navigate to the next level of their lives.

It's also important to understand that effort often goes unnoticed. It's not until we achieve success that people recognize us and frequently think we were overnight successes. This is far from the truth, so it's crucial to understand that loneliness is both okay and part of the process.

I'll end with this. There is no one you look up to who is super successful in what you are trying to accomplish that doesn't feel lonely at times. You are not a unicorn. I am sure Michael Jordan, J.K. Rowling, Jim Carrey, and Walt Disney sometimes felt lonely. You are in good company with some of the greats who applied the One Decision Away philosophy into their life and felt lonely, too. Just keep on going!

❸ *Key Takeaways*

1. **Loneliness Is Normal and Necessary for Growth**

   Feeling lonely is not only common but also a necessary part of pursuing big goals. It's a sign that you're stepping out of the crowd and striving for something extraordinary. Accept it as part of the process and embrace it as a phase you must grow through, not just go through.

2. **Be Your Own Hero and Cheerleader**

   On the journey to achieving your goals, external validation or encouragement will often be absent. Learn to motivate yourself by becoming your own hero. Talk to yourself positively, just as Dr. James Gills did, and remind yourself why you started in the first place. Your inner dialogue is your greatest tool.

3. **Effort Goes Unseen Before Success Is Celebrated**

   Understand that most of the work you put in will happen behind the scenes, unnoticed by others. Success is rarely recognized until it's achieved, but the perseverance and lonely nights you endure are the foundation of that success. Keep showing up even when no one is watching.

CHAPTER 8

Overcoming Procrastination

This is a huge obstacle. It is a huge obstacle that everyone on this earth has to overcome one way or another. We all procrastinate. Some are worse than others, but we all, at times, struggle with procrastination. Unfortunately, this is a dream killer. We often wait until we have more time or are less busy, but that never happens. We refuse to face the very thing we know we need to do because, at first, it is uncomfortable, and no one wants to be uncomfortable. The more time that goes by, the harder it becomes to decide to start, and eventually, that dream or goal gets buried so far away it gets forgotten about. But at some point, we will regret our choices. That little fire in our belly or tug at our heart will never truly go away. Unless you take action, it will haunt you for the rest of your life. You can try to bury it emotionally, but it will resurface at times and make you uncomfortable. Far too many people procrastinate in all areas of their life. We live in this gap of hesitation. The hesitation to get up on time. The hesitation to start that workout. The hesitation to send that email. The hesitation to start the work project. We live in this dangerous area of hesitation, which ultimately is the procrastination of our lives.

Through some research, I found some interesting information that I wanted to share with you about procrastination. First, the negative impact it has, and then I'll examine some strategies to help you overcome it.

PROCRASTINATION IS A DREAM KILLER.

One of the first studies on procrastination was published in the November 1997 edition of *Psychological Science*. Within it, researchers Dianne Tice and Roy Baumeister conducted a study at Case Western Reserve University where college students were rated on an established procrastination scale. Their academic performance was then tracked, and their stress and overall health throughout the semester was assessed. At first, it seemed as though there was a benefit to procrastination with lower levels of stress compared to others as a result of putting off schoolwork; however, that quickly changed. As time passed and the semester was nearing its end, the negative impact of procrastination far outweighed the positive. Lower grades were earned, and higher levels of cumulative stress were reported. Not only did the procrastinators finish work later, but the quality of their work and well-being suffered. This should remind you that refusing to be uncomfortable at first comes with a much higher price you will pay later on.

Furthermore, studies have found that procrastinators carry accompanying feelings of guilt, shame, or anxiety with their decision to delay. Conversely, as mentioned in Chapter 1, I once heard author, coach, and speaker Tony Robbins say progress is the #1 source of fulfillment. When we take action in our lives, it comes with great mental rewards. For example, think of how good it feels to finish simple errands or

REFUSING TO BE UNCOMFORTABLE AT FIRST COMES WITH A MUCH HIGHER PRICE YOU WILL PAY LATER ON.

your to-do list for that day. Why? You didn't procrastinate, and you took action. You got that dopamine release from the ventral tegmental area of your brain. It's all connected to making the one decision to move forward.

For me personally, losing my best friend, who was shot and killed in the line of duty as a young New York State Trooper, was all I needed to experience to understand every single day that life is a blessing and a gift. I refuse to procrastinate because I find gratitude each day and recognize we may not be here tomorrow. I know everyone may not experience such a tragedy in their life, but I can guarantee that you know someone, or know of someone, who died way too young. We are not bulletproof. The result for everyone on this earth is the same. We will all die at some point. I am not trying to be morbid, but I am trying to get you to think differently, change your mindset, and understand the only guaranteed day is today.

Timothy Pychyl and two Carleton University colleagues surveyed 119 students on procrastination before their midterm exams. In a 2010 issue of *Personality and Individual Differences* the research team reported that students who forgave themselves after procrastinating on the first exam were less likely to delay studying for the second one. What does this mean? Don't be so hard on yourself. If you have been putting something off for far too long, that's okay. Understand you are not alone. Many people struggle with the same thing. Remember, it's never too late to decide to start. It doesn't matter how old you are. You have breath. You have fresh air. You have a heartbeat. That means you can decide to start and get yourself back on track.

What you procrastinate on is different for everybody. Our lives are different. Our goals are different. Our careers are different. But at the root of procrastination, there are a lot of similarities, and here are a few ways you can overcome procrastination:

1) Set Clear Goals – Set concise goals and set a date on them. Most people don't set goals; if they do, they are too broad and don't put a date on it. Be specific. For example, as I write this book, I can say, "I want to write one new chapter weekly for the next 4 weeks." We need a date on it so we create urgency and must be specific so we can come up with an actionable plan.

2) Reverse Engineer Your Goals – If I want to write four chapters in the next 30 days, how much writing do I need to do each week? This will help me determine how much I need to write each day. Figure out your goal and work backward to formulate a daily operational plan.

3) Develop Good Habits – You must implement positive habits that align with your goals. In short, you must establish a routine that prepares you for success.

For me, waking up early and working out first thing in the morning is part of my routine. It's a habit I developed years ago that has become non-negotiable.

4) Block Out the Noise – Distractions are everywhere, and the #1 distraction is our phone. All the notifications dinging on your phone are enough to completely derail you because we get so focused on answering all the notifications. Turn off all the notifications on your phone. It has done wonders for me. Also, limit news consumption unless you want to be angry and stressed out constantly. I want to be informed but not consumed. This means I want to know what's happening in the world, but I am not looking to consume it all day like so many do, i.e., radio in the car, listening to the news, and listening to the news on the television at home.

5) Find an Accountability Partner – This can go for your career and personal life. Is there someone at work you can rely on and vice-versa? Develop that relationship with someone at work. As for your personal life, find a workout partner. Find someone who will keep you accountable to get your workouts in. Are you growing a business? Find someone who is also trying to build something and bounce ideas off each other. If you can't find anyone to work alongside with, I used the authors of the books I read as my mentors and accountability partners from afar. So much of my growth has been from people I had no direct contact with but applied what I learned from them. Having accountability to something or someone has many benefits.

6) Stay Positive – We all get knocked down at some point in our life. Trials and tribulations are all part of the journey of life. So, I recommend reading and/or listening to at least 10 minutes a day of a good self-help book or podcast so that you stay in a good head space. We must guard our minds like a prison. Feeding it some positivity each day will reap massive rewards in the end.

7) Just Start – Too many people wait until they feel like doing something before they start. We need to flip that upside down. Just start, and then you will begin to feel like it. Make that *one decision* to take that first step. Remember, no one is great at something the first time. We all have our own Day 1.

In summary, we all, at one time or another, know we procrastinate. But we don't need to live in this space and this gap of hesitation. Procrastination only leads to more grief later on. Make the *one decision* to move your life forward. If you are looking for a sign to start, this may be it. It's time to get back on the saddle, brush yourself off, and take massive action on your goals. What's the cost to your life by not committing to change? It's time.

❸ *Key Takeaways*

1. Procrastination Delays Progress and Increases Stress

The longer you delay acting, the harder it becomes to start, and the greater the toll it takes on your mental and emotional well-being. Remember, procrastination may feel easier in the short term, but the regret of unfulfilled potential will weigh heavier in the long term.

2. Action Is the Antidote to Procrastination

Progress starts with simply *one decision* – just start. Don't wait until you feel ready or motivated; instead, take action, and the momentum will follow with that feel good dopamine release. Even small steps toward your goal will build confidence and a sense of fulfillment.

3. Practical Tools to Combat Procrastination

- Set clear, specific goals with deadlines to create urgency.
- Reverse-engineer your goals into daily, actionable steps.
- Block distractions like unnecessary phone notifications and limit media consumption.
- Build habits and routines that support your success, like starting your day with purpose.

CHAPTER 9

Facing Your Fears

think it's super important that after the chapter on procrastination, I discuss facing our fears. For some, it's the fear of failure. They are afraid to try new things and grow. For others, it's the fear of success. They are scared they won't be able to handle their life if they reach their goals. Either way, it stops people from making the decision to start. Let's talk about the acronym of F.E.A.R. – **F**alse **E**vidence **A**ppearing **R**eal. It's often made up in our minds, and 99 percent of the things you worry about will never actually come to fruition. Yet, you let it stop you.

One of our biggest fears is worrying about what other people may think of us. You must remind yourself that other people's opinions of you are not your reality. Read that sentence twice. Far too many of us don't decide to take that first step because we are worried about what our friend, co-worker, mom, or dad may think of us. These people have struggles in their lives and are not thinking about you nearly as much as you are worrying about them. So let that fear go and stop giving someone power over your life. The most freeing feeling in the world is when you learn to not care about what other people think of you and understand that you alone own your life.

I think it's important to note that I am not trying to tell you to get rid of all your fears, or that it's not a real thing we experience. We all have fear. I have fears, too. But it takes one word to be able to overcome our fears. Just one simple word to help us decide to move forward. That word is courage. We need the courage to make the *one decision* not to let fear stop us. We all need to muster up some courage at some point in life so we can live to our fullest potential and experience all that life has to offer.

I love President Franklin D. Roosevelt's quote, "The only thing we have to fear is fear itself." Why? Because you miss 100 percent of the shots you don't take so, if you let fear stop you from taking action, then it's the actual fear that you need to be most concerned about.

Do you experience an intense fear of failure? If so, do not worry. It's called atychiphobia, and many face this. It may cause you to put off or avoid any activity or scenario that has the potential for an unsuccessful outcome. You may be scared to try new things, take risks, or embrace growth for fear of failure. Do you feel fear has been an excuse of yours lately? Are you unsure if it's stopping you from moving forward? In a Cleveland Clinic article about atychiphobia, they list that people with a fear of failure may be:

- Afraid of performing simple tasks at work, home, or school.
- Angry or irritable.
- Anxious about being judged by others.

- Depressed or sad.
- Pessimistic (negative outlook on life).
- Prone to procrastination if a task or activity seems challenging.
- Unable to maintain relationships.
- Unwilling to accept constructive criticism or help.

Sometimes, the fear of failure may cause people to avoid trying altogether. Because they are so afraid that they will try and not succeed, they decide not to try at all to prevent potential pain, embarrassment, or disappointment. But I know later, they will regret not trying. The struggle is less painful than regret. So, even if you deal with some pain, embarrassment, or disappointment, remember it won't kill you. What may kill you is the mental anguish from the regret you will have later for not trying. Next time you feel afraid, take a deep breath and ask yourself these questions:

- What am I really afraid of? If it helps, write down your answers. Problems look much smaller when we actually get to the root of what we fear.

- Who am I fighting for? What is your why? Sometimes, when we attach a why to something bigger than ourselves, we don't want to disappoint them, so we take the necessary steps to move forward – more about this in a later chapter.

- What's the worst that could happen? The worst-case scenario may not be as bad as you think. In many cases, failure doesn't change much about your current situation, so what do you have to lose?

What if I succeed? Instead of thinking why it won't work, change your mindset to what if you actually did it. What if you succeeded? How would that make you feel? Who would you impact positively?

THE STRUGGLE IS LESS PAINFUL THAN REGRET.

What if I do fail? I'm sure this isn't a life-and-death situation, so sometimes we need to take a step back and give ourselves some life perspective. Is this going to end or ruin our life? Most times, the answer is no, but we let our minds spiral out of control as if our lives will end if we fail.

Here are some tips you can use to help overcome some of your fears:

1) Understand Failure Is Normal — Everyone fails at some point in life, and failure is probably the best way to learn. We never learn anything new when things go right, but it's when things go wrong that we can learn so much from. So, accept failure as part of the process of growing.

2) Keep a Beginner's Mindset — No one is great at anything the first time they do it. Michael Phelps was not the greatest swimmer of all time the first time he jumped in the pool. It took a lot of hard work and many lessons of failure for him to grow. Understand that nothing is easy the first time, and it takes patience and many failures along the way to become great at something.

3) Talk With Someone – I often bounce ideas, worries, or concerns off my wife. She is my sounding board, and I always appreciate her feedback. I have even used my therapist to help me navigate specific concerns or fears. The point is, don't bundle all your worries up internally. Talk to a friend or significant other about it and get some outside perspective.

4) Remember the Cost of Regret – This is my biggest fear, and it helps me overcome any current fears. You miss 100 percent of the shots you don't take, and you can guarantee one thing if you aren't willing to try: failure. Do not live with regret.

5) You Can Make Adjustments – I cannot count the number of times I was worried about something happening and something different happened. Either way, you can make adjustments along the way. You adapt and overcome.

6) Accept the Fear, But Do It Anyway – As mentioned above, all we need is a little bit of courage to move forward. You may not be able to eliminate the fear, but do it anyway. Make the decision to face your fear.

In summary, I want you to picture this. You are lying on your deathbed many years from now and looking down at you are the ghosts of your talents, your dreams, and your ideas, and they are yelling, "I came to you, but because of fear, you didn't give me life." My question to you then is are these dreams and talents going to die with you, or are you going to make the *decision* and give them life? Have just a little bit of courage, my friends. Be willing to make that decision to face your fears and level up your life.

🔑 Key Takeaways

1. Fear Is Mostly an Illusion

Fear is often just **F**alse **E**vidence **A**ppearing **R**eal. Most of the things we fear or worry about never actually happen. Recognize that fear is usually a mental barrier, not a reality, and don't let it stop you from taking action.

2. Failure Is a Stepping-Stone, Not the End

Failure is a normal part of growth and one of life's greatest teachers. You're not supposed to be perfect on your first try — no one is. Embrace failure as part of the process and let it propel you forward instead of holding you back.

3. Courage Is the Key to Overcoming Fear

You don't need to eliminate fear entirely to move forward. I often share on stage that all it takes is a small moment of courage to face your fears and make the decision to act. The cost of regret is far greater than the temporary discomfort of fear — so feel the fear, and do it anyway.

CHAPTER 10

STOP Comparing Yourself to Others

One of the biggest reasons why so many people don't make the decision to move forward and go after their goals and dreams is because they compare themselves to others. Focusing on others and comparing yourself to them is a cancer to your contentment and satisfaction. I want to share a story with you that paints this picture.

In 2023, I planned to run the New York City Marathon with the goal of beating my younger self. I ran this race twice before. The last time was 16 years earlier. I followed the training precisely as prescribed. I didn't miss

FOCUSING ON OTHERS AND COMPARING YOURSELF TO THEM IS A CANCER TO YOUR CONTENTMENT AND SATISFACTION.

a day, even when my travel schedule for speaking picked up. At the peak of my training, which meant I ran about 4 days during the week (averaging 6 miles per run) and one long run on the weekend (averaging about 18 miles), I had nine keynote speaking events in just 6 weeks. But I never missed a day. If it meant I had to run 8 miles on a hotel treadmill after speaking for an hour on stage, I did it. I was committed. I did everything right.

Then came Marathon Sunday in New York City, a day like no other in New York. There are millions of spectators, and the energy you feel is something I wish I could bottle up and experience again later. The race started, and I cruised along for the first half of the race. I was on pace to beat my older time, and I felt great. Around mile 14 of the 26.2-mile race, I began getting cramps in my right calf. It spread to my right quad. Then, to my entire left leg as well. Then it even spread into my back and right forearm. I couldn't believe

what was happening after all the training I did. I was in tears of pain as I battled hundreds of cramping episodes throughout the remaining 12 miles, but I was committed to finishing. I finished, but I was broken internally.

A picture of me smiling after I crossed the finish line holding my medal was taken, as seen here. Based on what you saw, you would have thought I was happy and proud of my accomplishment.

But that couldn't be farther from the truth. For 2 days, I continued to feel broken internally. I was depressed because I did everything right, but my body shut down that day. I shared that picture of me smiling and holding my medal on social media and received many positive comments. But here is the thing. Do not compare the highlight reel you see on social media to your everyday life. There are way too many people who compare their everyday struggles to the highlight reel people are only willing to share on social media. For me, you would think life was great with the big smile on my face in that picture, but that could not have been farther from the truth. The overwhelming majority of people never share their struggles on social media. But even when struggling, their posts often reflect nothing other than happiness. Do not fall into this trap. Do not compare your daily challenges to the non-authentic fake things you see on social media. Everyone does it, and we need to recognize that it's not serving us and is not the truth.

DO NOT COMPARE THE HIGHLIGHT REEL YOU SEE ON SOCIAL MEDIA TO YOUR EVERYDAY LIFE.

We continue to do this throughout our day. For example, you may see a red sports car speeding down the highway and think about how awesome it must be to be that person. You may wish you had that car and that life, too. But what you don't know is that maybe that person just lost their job that supported his/her family, and they are contemplating suicide. Or maybe that person just broke up from a long-term relationship and feels completely isolated and alone. Or perhaps that person is struggling with a sickness or disease. You don't know, so you cannot make assumptions.

Money isn't everything, either. Remember, some very wealthy people are miserable and feel isolated and lonely all the time. Some wealthy people are completely stressed out because of the burden that comes with being super wealthy in business. Maybe they have a thousand employees they have to support and have the weight of that responsibility on their shoulders. Or they are dealing with the fact that the decisions they make or don't make can affect large numbers of people. They don't just report to work and then come home. People who are wealthy often have a lot more weighing on their shoulders. Yes, the money may be great, but with that comes a lot more stress. You don't know what someone else is dealing with. We all have problems and things we need to face.

You are unique and different from everyone else. You are from a different family, from a different culture, and have different abilities. So, the only person you should compare yourself to is yourself. My daily goal is to strive to be better than I was yesterday. That is it. I cannot compare myself to others because they live a completely different life. They are entirely different people, and they have completely different goals and dreams.

THE ONLY PERSON YOU SHOULD COMPARE YOURSELF TO IS YOURSELF.

I mentioned this in my first book, *The Leveled Up Life*, but it is essential to bring it up again. If you need to unfollow, block, unfriend, snooze, disconnect, etc., someone because you look up to them and you find yourself comparing yourself to them, then so be it. I have done this before because it is a distraction and outside noise. It is not serving me. You need to run your race. Not theirs. I am unique in my own way. Comparing myself to someone else will generate negative self-talk, which is unacceptable in my book. I suggest you do the same.

It is also important to understand the danger of comparing yourself to your peers. It's so easy to feel like that coworker, friend, or acquaintance who tells you how great everything is going for them is better than you. But the reality is 99 percent of people aren't willing to share their struggles and be vulnerable. We all struggle. No one is immune to it, but few are willing to share it. Focus on being the best you can be and not being so concerned with what others are doing. It never serves you. Run your race.

Except for a very small percentage of people, there is no such thing as an overnight success. Every successful person you compare yourself to has been doing it much longer than you think. No one sees the thousands of hours of work it took for that person to get there. They only see the success they have today. As mentioned earlier in the book, effort goes unnoticed. It's not until someone is successful that they get recognized.

In the end, do not allow comparison to stop you from making the decision to start and move forward. People too often give up before they even begin because we compare ourselves to false realities. You need to stop doing that. Please run your race. This is your life. Your journey. Don't let the obstacle of comparison derail you from deciding to focus on being the best you can be. When we make the proper decisions to move forward and experience positive progress in our own lives, we cannot allow one social media post, someone else's success, or some fake happiness we see online derail us. It's your journey. It's your life. Honor it. Embrace it. Own it. Make the *one decision*. Move forward.

③ *Key Takeaways*

1. **Recognize the Illusion of Social Media**

   People often share only the highlights of their lives online, which can create a distorted perception of reality. Remember that these curated images don't reflect the full spectrum of their experiences. Avoid comparing your everyday life to someone else's highlight reel.

2. **Focus on Your Personal Journey**

   Everyone's path is unique and shaped by different backgrounds, challenges, and goals. Instead of measuring your progress against others, concentrate on your own growth and strive to be better than you were yesterday.

3. **Limit Exposure to Triggers**

   Identify situations or platforms that prompt you to compare yourself to others, such as certain social media accounts. Consider unfollowing or muting accounts that negatively impact your self-esteem. By reducing exposure to these triggers, you can maintain a healthier mindset.

   By internalizing these principles, you can cultivate a more positive self-image and stay committed to your personal development without the burden of comparison.

CHAPTER 11

Let the Past Go

There is a reason why the front windshield is bigger than the rearview mirror. It's because you're not going that way. Yet far too many people are stuck in the past. They haven't decided to move forward in their life because they are stuck living in their past. As the world evolves, we cling onto every ounce of hope, waiting for things to change and returning to the way things used to be. That never happens. How often do you hear someone say, "Back in the day ... ?" Unfortunately, time waits for no one, and rarely, if ever, do things revert to the old days. Furthermore, you may be holding onto a grudge towards someone for something that happened many years ago. Many obstacles hold people back from making the decision to move forward, but some other not so obvious ones hold people back. For example, some people hold onto security now, no matter how miserable they may be, at the expense of potentially missing out on something more significant in their lives later. Sometimes obstacles overlap, but in the end, they all require the same thing. Making the decision to let go and move forward.

Living in the past is a death sentence to a better life. It keeps people paralyzed from doing anything because all they talk and think about is their past. They are stuck talking about the highlights of their high school or college days as if they can never create new highlights for their life. For some, yes, these were great times. For others, they are full of trials and tribulations. But in the end, the same answer applies. It doesn't matter. We cannot change the past. It's finite. It's over. But we must understand that every day we wake up, we are given another chance. We are handed a new, clean slate. God is not through with us yet. What you choose to do today can be a new masterpiece of art for an even better life, or you can stay stuck and live in your past. You must be willing to let the past go. It's not serving you anymore.

We may need to let go of something good to go after something great. Simply put, we must give up the good to go for the great! In 2020, I was at a pivotal point in my state police career after 22 years of service. I was a captain at the time, running all state police operations for the County of Westchester, New York. I had a great career and loved all the people I worked with. It's a camaraderie like no other being in a career where people will put their lives on the line for you. Up until this point, I accomplished many great things in my career. I was involved in everything you could imagine and saw enough tragedy for multiple lifetimes. Other than getting promoted again, there wasn't much left I truly wanted to achieve. The next thing on my radar was getting promoted to the rank of Major, which was appealing, but as much as I enjoyed my job, something was missing. At this point in my life, I was not only working full-time with the state police, but my direct sales business also demanded a lot of effort and work. By this point in my career, I had spoken to groups of 1000 plus at my direct sales events for over 10 years. It culminated to an audience of 20,000 in the NFL Super Dome at our annual conference. After speaking to the group of 20,000, I had a conversation that changed my life. As mentioned earlier in this book, as I exited the bathroom backstage in the NFL Super Dome, an executive within the company who just heard me speak asked me if I ever thought of being a keynote speaker. He pointed out how impactful my message was and my ability to speak to so many people comfortably on such a big stage. I never thought about doing this. I knew I enjoyed sharing my message on stage, but as a paid professional speaker? No, it never crossed my mind. This executive insisted I consider doing it. But here was the bigger problem. I was a busy dad of three daughters and a husband, running all state police operations for an entire county, and also had a very busy direct sales business with a team of 1,400 people. How could I find any more time to add more to my plate? The answer was simple. I couldn't.

But after that seed was planted in my mind, I felt something in my gut telling me I needed to pursue this. It wouldn't go away.

I also believe that God gives every one of us gifts, and we are all born with them. Your gift is the thing you do best with the least amount of effort. What is that for you? My first opportunity to speak and the praise I received after my presentations opened my eyes to a gift I had never

WE MAY NEED TO LET GO OF SOMETHING GOOD TO GO AFTER SOMETHING GREAT.

known I had. That was public speaking. Another example is my wife, who is an unbelievable natural cook. She can put together some of the best food I've ever tasted with minimal effort. I watch in awe how she whips together a delicious meal without thinking. I can barbecue and make pancakes. That's about it! Ha! But the point is we all have gifts, and I was at a point in my life where a new door was opening for me. I have always understood to follow my gut and decide to go through whatever new doors are presented to me. But this didn't come without a price tag attached to it. I knew the only way I would be able to do this was if I retired from the state police so I could pursue being a professional keynote motivational speaker. This was beyond scary for me. I was only 43 years old. I was looking to get promoted from captain to major in the foreseeable future. I anticipated working in law enforcement for over 30 years, like many do. It was a secure job. I worked with some of the best people, many of whom were close friends. I loved the New York State Police agency, and part of me didn't want to let go.

Like I said before, sometimes in our lives, we need to give up the good and go for the great. I accomplished so much in my state police career, but I was now presented with an opportunity to do something even more significant in my life and use my story and my voice to impact thousands of people in this world. I once read that for a man to gain his life, he must first lose his life. You must be willing to let who you are now die to give birth to who you can become. This is very profound and so very true.

This fork in the road of my life was upon me, and I needed to decide on what to do next. I decided to do an exercise with myself on the way to work to help me make up my mind and decide. I knew I needed to listen to my gut, but I still had hesitation and doubts, so I decided to do this exercise to get to the root of my concerns. Let me share it with you. As I was driving to work, I asked myself to list out in my head all the reasons I wanted to stay exactly where I was with the state police. What was holding me back? I needed to get to the root of my self-doubt, like peeling back the layers of an onion to get to the issue's core. In the end, it came down to one thing. I did not want to leave the people. I did not want to stop seeing the people I worked with and had such great relationships with. Once I determined this, a light bulb moment came over me. Whether I stayed on the state police for 30 years or whether I retired now at 22 years, at some point, I would need to leave the people. I would have to walk away. Once I realized this, my decision was made. It was time to retire. It was time to give up the good and go for the great. It was time for me to let go of my current life to go after and gain my next one. But this didn't come without paying a price.

You need to know that this was extremely hard to do. It was mentally draining and very emotional. I was scared. I had doubts. Many people didn't support me. Others negatively criticized me. It was harder than I anticipated, and I had minimal support. However, I wouldn't let this stop me. I leaned into the personal growth from the books I read, my increased faith in God, and the fear that if I didn't decide to pursue this, I would regret it later on. If you are at a point in your life where you, too, find yourself in a similar situation, it's time to let go of your security rope as well. Don't expect it to be easy. It will be ten times harder than you could ever imagine. The person you are right now will not get you to the goals you want to reach tomorrow. You are going to have to go through a growth journey. But if you follow your gut, listen to the whispers, lean into your gifts, and pair it with undeniable faith, it will work out. Proverbs 18:16 says, *"Your gift will make room for you."* I firmly believe this, but it starts with making the decision.

I ultimately made the decision and retired the week after the 2020 US Open for golf, where I was the incident commander for this event, which took over 2 years of planning. It was at the famous and iconic Winged Foot Golf Club. I wanted to see this through as it was delayed earlier in the year. However, it came with a hefty price tag. The last 6 months of my career were stressful and brutal. Ground zero for the coronavirus was in the county I ran, and the State of New York was losing over 500 people daily. I set up and ran the first national testing site in New Rochelle, NY. When I got home from work, my wife wouldn't allow me in the house until I stripped down to nothing in our cold garage out of fear of bringing the virus into our home. We didn't know what it was and what we were dealing with at the time. Additionally, all the protests were unfolding from the George Floyd incident earlier that year. The State Police frequently got called to assist local law enforcement agencies with protests. I personally was getting death threats and hate messages through my social media channels that I had for years from building my online direct sales business. I feared for my family and even for my own life. Putting gas in my police car while in uniform had me constantly looking over my shoulder out of fear of getting ambushed. However, I never say I will do something and not finish. Not seeing the US Open through, that I spent so much time planning for wasn't an option. My wife even at times told me to retire. That is was not worth what I was going through. But quitting or giving up was not an option. Finishing what I started was my only option. Far too many people start things and don't finish. To me, it not only impacts you, but it will negatively impact those around you that you touch. For example, some people relied on me for the US Open, and I wasn't about to leave them hanging. After a lot of long hours and stress, it all worked out. I finally let go of my security rope to pursue the next chapter of my life.

Life has a funny way of challenging you even more when you set out to do something. I faced a new dilemma as I began this new chapter. It felt as if this was Phase II of giving up the good of the state police to go for the great as a speaker. Each day, I was trying to continue to actively grow my direct sales business while also pursuing a new dream business of being a speaker, and it just didn't work. A few years back, I was in the audience at an event listening to my favorite author and leadership expert, John Maxwell, speak, and he asked us all a question. He asked, "If there was a large tree in the forest and every day you hit the same tree five times, what would ultimately happen?" The answer would be it would fall. But then he asked us, "What would happen if, over time, you hit five different trees only one time?" The answer would be that you would have a scarred forest. The point was that you can't do more than one thing really well. Something will suffer. You need to focus on one tree and work at it daily with all your effort and time. While I began to feel the stress of trying to build two businesses, I started paying attention to the changing signs of my direct sales business. For one, the company focused on new programs and products primarily meant for women. Second, the overwhelming majority of top leaders in the company were female. These ladies were doing amazing things, and they deserved success. My wife Kristen was one of them. Third, the company has also struggled overall for the last few years, especially since it became a publicly traded stock. But that's not my point here. My point was that I was trying to continue to build a business, but right out of the gate, I was up against heavy resistance, trying to share and sell products that I couldn't identify with and for a company that was struggling. I again needed to let go of the good to go for the great. I needed to let go of this chapter of my life regarding business. I didn't quit or completely give up on it. It was reallocating my time and effort to one place instead of two. This had its own share of mental challenges. The biggest was the financial security it provided for my family and the effort it took to maintain the income. So, I once again had to lean into my faith.

You have to follow your gut. You have to listen to the whispers. You need to let the past go. You need to make the *one decision* at that moment to go all in on the new area of your life. No hesitation. Just make the decision and understand your gift will make room for you, as mentioned above in Proverbs 18:16.

> **YOU HAVE TO LISTEN TO THE WHISPERS. YOU NEED TO LET THE PAST GO.**

Another element of letting the past go applies to so many of us. That is the element of forgiveness. There may be someone in your life who wronged you, which is holding you back from making the decision to move your life forward. It may be so bad that you don't even want to talk to or see the person again. Let me share some insight with you to help you understand forgiveness. Sometimes in life, we aren't forgiving someone to free and help them, but rather, we are forgiving someone so we can stop letting that person have power over us for what they did. You may need to read that twice. Forgiveness is not for them. It is for you. One of the worst things we can allow in our lives is for someone to have power and control over us. To allow someone else to impact the choices we make going forward in our own life. This is not a place to live. We are being held hostage by that person. So, it may be time for you to forgive that person for whatever they did so you can release the tension holding you back from living the life you were meant to live. I like to say, "Bless and release." This is not intended to be easy but to help you heal and move you forward. You deserve the freedom to make your own decisions without someone else holding you back.

Everyone's situation and life is different, but no matter what your past is, I know living in it will not serve your future. You must be willing to decide right now to let the past go. You are *one decision away*. Only you will know what that means and what it looks like for you. Yes, you can still have all the memories in your mind, but you cannot let them control you and prevent you from deciding on a brighter future for your tomorrow. Focus forward. Focus on today. Focus on what's in front of you. You are *one decision away* from making that shift. It starts today.

❸ Key Takeaways

1. The Rearview Mirror Principle

Living in your past prevents forward progress. Your past is unchangeable, but every day is a chance to create new memories and achievements. Focus on the opportunities in front of you, not the chapters you've already written.

2. Give Up Good for Great

Pursue your gut instincts and follow the new doors that open in your life, even when it means leaving behind comfort or security. Growth often requires sacrifice, but it's the path to something greater and more fulfilling.

3. Forgiveness Is Freedom

Forgiving someone doesn't excuse their actions but releases their power over you. Let go of grudges to free yourself from the chains of resentment and create space for personal freedom and growth.

CHAPTER 12

Don't Overcomplicate It

ne of the worst things that we do as a society today is we tend to overcomplicate things. Everything we do takes us twice as long because we allow all the outside noise to distract us. Before I go any further, I think it's important again to give you my definition of the One Decision Away philosophy, *"It's a choice made in the present moment backed by courage and faith to move you one step closer to your goals."* In short, it's the sole decision you make in the present moment. It doesn't say it is backed by other's opinions, social media, or anything else. It is a simple state of being to move our lives forward, one decision at a time. However, we need to discuss the most common obstacles that cause us to overcomplicate this simple philosophy.

The medium at the center of this problem is our cell phones. As great as it is, with technological advancements, it has also become problematic. It is a distraction and puts obstacles right in our way from moving forward in our lives. Let me give you an example. You finally decide to start exercising again, and your goal is to go to the gym 3 times a week and take classes after work. You are about to sign up on the gym website, but instead, you check your Instagram quickly. As soon as you open your Instagram, you see a video discussing why exercising in the morning is better for you. Furthermore, you scroll down a bit more and see ads for calisthenic workouts that help you lose belly fat that you can do from home for just $1.99. You immediately start questioning your original decision, so instead of signing up at your gym, you do nothing because you are second-guessing yourself. That's how quickly social media can distract you and cause you to complicate such a simple decision. Go online to your gym and sign up.

Don't forget that your cell phone tracks everything you do and puts more of what you have been searching for in your newsfeed. When you click on an ad about exercise, you see more posts about exercise. You click on pictures of farmhouses you like and see more posts with farmhouses. You look at a new television online at Best Buy and now have Best Buy ads running on your social media. We are constantly bombarded with information, which ultimately causes too many of us to do nothing. We have paralysis of analysis. It's an endless cycle of procrastination. Furthermore, we make up our minds with the decision to do something, and before we know it, we are scrolling and watching mindless social media videos for hours. We lose countless hours of our lives. Studies by the Global Marketing Industry say the average person spends 2 hours and 23 minutes daily on social media. The average time we spend watching television is 3 hours. That is over 5 hours a day, equating to 35 hours a week. Almost a whole workweek! Imagine where we could be if we instead used that time to be more efficient and do the things we know we need to get done. You don't need more time. You are not too busy. You need to adjust your priorities in your life.

The next reason you fail to make the simple decision to move forward is that you let other people's opinions affect you. When I started my direct sales business with Beachbody, many people told me it was a pyramid scheme, that multi-level marketing businesses don't work, that I was wasting my time, and so on. This even happened when I wanted to retire from the state police. Everyone wants to share their opinion with you, and far too often, we let some person get in our heads who has zero experience in what we are trying to accomplish. Here is my advice for you. Only take constructive criticism from someone more successful than you. It's that simple. If you want to take it one step further, only accept constructive criticism from someone more successful than you in the area you want to improve. Everyone else's opinions do not matter.

The One Decision Away philosophy is genuinely that simple. It's a state of being within ourselves to wake up each day and keep moving the needle forward. We cannot allow outside sources to stop us. However, at times, we can get in our own way. Too often, we want to ensure we have everything in place before deciding to start. We spend hours and hours dotting our "i's" and crossing our "t's" instead of just starting. I have learned that we cannot wait for everything to be perfectly in place before we start. We must start, and then we will figure everything else out. It seems backwards, but it works. Don't wait for the motivation to start. Start, and then you will create the motivation to keep going. Remember, taking action to start creates progress. Progress generates fulfillment, which feels good. How? Dopamine releases in our brains.

DON'T WAIT FOR THE MOTIVATION TO START. START, AND THEN YOU WILL CREATE THE MOTIVATION TO KEEP GOING.

I always loved the acronym K.I.S.S. (keep it simple, stupid). Why? Because it's true! We need to focus forward each day. Today, when I woke up, I immediately decided to go through my morning routine of meditation, prayer, and exercise. From there, I decided to continue to write this book – no social media, no television, no news, no phone calls, etc. I refused to allow outside distractions to complicate my life. We need to keep it simple.

I genuinely believe we overcomplicate everything in our lives today when it doesn't need to be that complicated. Yes, our phones are to blame, but at the end of the day, we control our actions. We control how we respond to everything in our life. There comes a time when you need to learn to center yourself and not allow outside forces to control your life. Will it be easy? No, it won't. But we must learn to understand that everyone's life is different, and we cannot allow someone else's experience in their life impact the choices and decisions we make about ours. Keep it simple. One day at a time. One hour at a time. One minute at a time. One second at a time. Make the *one decision*. It's right there in front of you. You know what you need to do.

🔑 Key Takeaways

1. Limit Distractions and Take Immediate Action

Don't let outside noise – like social media or excessive opinions – derail your progress. Make your decision and act on it without second-guessing or overanalyzing. Remember, your phone is a tool, not a barrier. Use it wisely to enhance your focus, not distract from it.

2. Focus on Constructive Input Only

Only take advice from people who are more successful than you in the area you want to improve. Block out opinions that don't add value or are rooted in negativity. Stay aligned with your own goals and trust your instincts.

3. Start Now, Adjust as You Go

Stop waiting for the perfect moment or all the answers before starting. Perfection isn't a prerequisite for progress. Begin today, keep it simple, and trust that the momentum you create will build motivation and clarity along the way.

PART 3

TOOLS TO APPLY THE ONE DECISION AWAY PHILOSOPHY

In this part of the book, I want to review all the tools you will need to help you apply the One Decision Away philosophy in your life. The prior chapters reminded you of the most common obstacles that will get in your way, but now it's time to talk about principles that will help you overcome them. Yes, there are challenges. Yes, there will be setbacks. We cannot control what happens to us, but we can control how we react. Therefore, we can choose how to respond, and if you can follow some of the principles I share with you in the following chapters, you will have great success. It's time to get to work!

WE CANNOT CONTROL WHAT HAPPENS TO US, BUT WE CAN CONTROL HOW WE REACT.

CHAPTER 13

Vision

Everything starts with having a vision for our life. Without it, nothing will motivate us or pull us towards a better life. Without a vision, we cannot leverage the power of the One Decision Away philosophy because nothing is pulling us towards something better. It's important to understand that humans have one thing that no other living form has, and its the ability to have an imagination. No other creature or animal can create an imagination. I am grateful to know this. For humans, what we see with our eyes is called sight. But what we can see with our minds is called insight. We as humans must embrace our brains ability to imagine, dream, and have that vision for a more extraordinary life.

WHAT WE SEE WITH OUR EYES IS CALLED SIGHT. BUT WHAT WE CAN SEE WITH OUR MINDS IS CALLED INSIGHT.

Up until now, you are the product of the choices and decisions you made up to this point. Whether you like where you are or not, you are here based on how you've shown up each day. You can try to blame your circumstances, but in the end, you have complete control over how you react to what happened to you. So, your past life's decisions led you to a vision you liked or did not like. Ask yourself, are you enjoying where you are right now? If not, that's okay. If you are, great, but there is always room to experience an even more fulfilled life.

What are your goals? What are your dreams? Where do you want to be in 3 months from now? How about 6 months from now? A year from now? Having clarity is at the core of having a powerful vision, but you must make that one decision and start taking action. There is no warm-up in life. There is no practice in life. All we have is today. Don't waste any more time.

Sometimes in life, we need to be our own hero. Supporting your goals or dreams is no one else's job but our own. It's on you as an individual to decide to make that happen. Want to start that new hobby? Do it. Want to start that new career? Do it. Want to start that new business you always dreamed of? Do it. The only thing stopping you from going after the vision is the *one decision* to start. It will never be the perfect moment or the perfect time to start. It's about creating it.

Let me remind you that it's okay if it doesn't go perfectly. It's okay if the pursuit of your vision takes a detour or goes on some scenic route. The important thing is that you know where you are going. You cannot just wake up and go through the motions. That is not a way to live. That is merely existing. If you merely exist, you may make the wrong career choice or get involved in the wrong relationship. A vision creates a clear path for our life.

So, at some point, you need to make the decision to just do it. It will be a tough decision and won't be easy, but you need to take the leap of faith. I had to decide to retire from the New York State Police to pursue a new vision for my future. The new vision was to make a more significant impact by serving and speaking to thousands of people as a speaker. I initially served the people of the State of New York as a State Trooper, but this was more significant. I then made the decision to write my first book. Then, the decision to write a second book. We are always *one decision away* from moving the needle in our lives. But we cannot sit on the sidelines of our lives forever. You must get down on the ball field and get in the game.

It doesn't matter who doesn't see or agree with your vision. As long as you see it, then that's all that matters. Don't wait for approval from others. Don't wait for someone to give you permission to go after your vision. It was placed in your mind for a reason. Not someone else's. Then, remind yourself of that vision every day when you wake up because life will try to derail you. Life will challenge you. Life will throw you curveballs you didn't see coming. However, it's the power of your vision that pulls you through.

I can tell if someone has a strong vision without them even saying it. You will see it in their actions. They will have discipline. They will have drive. They will have consistency. They are relentless in their pursuit to make their vision become a reality. They become obsessed with their goals. Those without a vision wake up each day hoping to survive with whatever life throws at them. They count down the days to the weekend. Sunday nights are miserable. You see them walking all over, head down, shoulders hunched, just meandering through life. This is not a way to live.

About a week ago, I met an ultramarathoner and very successful businessman, Joe Gagnon. He is the author of *Living the High Performance Life: An Average Joe's Guide to the Extraordinary*. He's done over 60 ultramarathons and many other races. He told me about a point in his life when he turned 40 years old and became financially successful, but he asked himself, "Is this it? Is this all that life is about?" It wasn't until then that he decided to cast a vision for a more fulfilled and impactful life. He was very successful financially, so he started pursuing a healthier life. He started exercising and testing his abilities. He went from a few days a week to a few more, ultimately becoming an elite athlete exercising 7 days a week. He ran six marathons in 6 days on six different continents. Today, he strives to give back to the world and serve others through his philanthropic work. He even helped me identify the first ultramarathon that I had decided to do. He is an absolute legend in my book but, more importantly, the epitome of having a vision for your life. You are never too old to start. It is never too late to create a new vision for your life. Just like Joe, the key is to make the one decision to start.

IT IS NEVER TOO LATE TO CREATE A NEW VISION FOR YOUR LIFE.

Some people like creating vision boards where they print out pictures of their dreams and hang them up so they see them every day. Some people like writing their visions out so they can read them daily to remind themselves why they are doing the hard work. Some people have wallpapers on their devices with inspiring quotes to keep them motivated to keep going after their vision. It doesn't matter what you decide to do, but those with a vision are intentional with their life. They are conscious of the vision they want for their future, and they have an action plan in place. They do not just wing it. They have structure. They have a routine. They developed habits that have become non-negotiable in their life that move them closer to their goals. They review their vision daily. It's at the forefront of their mind. As I look to my left, hanging on the wall in my office, I see a black and white picture of a boardwalk leading to a beach taken from a beach house. That's part of my vision for the future; I look at it every day.

Before you finish this chapter, sit with yourself for a while and think. Go for a walk. No distractions. No music. No phone. Ask yourself, what are your goals? What are your dreams? What would your life look like if you had all the money and time in the world? I want you to dream again. I want you to thrive again. I want you to feel a sense of purpose again. I want you to feel fulfilled. I want you to feel joy. It all starts with having a vision and making the *one decision* to start. You got this.

❸ Key Takeaways

1. Your Vision Is Your Compass

A clear vision gives your life direction and purpose. Without it, you're merely existing rather than truly living. Use your imagination to create a vision for the life you want, and let it pull you forward every day.

ACTIONABLE EXERCISE

Set aside 10-15 minutes today to create a detailed vision for your life. Write down where you want to be in the next 3-5 years in areas like career, health, relationships, and personal growth. Be as specific as possible, and review this vision weekly to stay on track.

2. The Power of One Decision

Achieving your vision begins with one decision to start. Stop waiting for the "perfect time" because it doesn't exist. Take action today, even if it's a small step, and trust that the path will unfold as you move forward.

ACTIONABLE EXERCISE

Write down one small but meaningful action you can take today to move closer to your vision. Whether it's sending an email, making a phone call, or setting up a plan, commit to doing it before the day ends. Repeat this process daily.

3. Keep Your Vision Alive Daily

Review your vision every day to stay focused and motivated. Whether through a vision board, written goals, or inspiring reminders, keep your dreams at the forefront of your mind. Let your daily actions align with your vision, and never let life's challenges derail you.

ACTIONABLE EXERCISE

Create a morning routine where you spend 5 minutes reviewing your vision. This could include looking at your vision board, reading your written goals, or visualizing yourself achieving them. Reflect on one action you can take that day to bring you closer to your goals.

When the Unexpected Happens

This book is taking a slight detour after some unexpected personal events happened in my life, literally in the middle of writing it. Just after I finished writing the last chapter, we received some bad news. This wasn't the plan for Chapter 14, but what I am about to share with you is the epitome of the One Decision Away philosophy.

It was September 30th, 2024, around 5:15 p.m., when my wife and I heard rumblings that Beachbody, the company we were coaches with for over 14 years, was shutting down the coach network. This meant that our large direct sales team of 1,400 people we built from the ground up, the income that supported my family, and the thousands and thousands of clients we had might be taken away from us. Unfortunately, the sad reality was that it was true. The CEO of the company made a live video and announced that they were dissolving and shutting down the direct sales arm of the company and that they will be going to an affiliate business model within weeks. There was no warning.

This meant the income my wife and I relied on for my family was being taken away. The changes were happening in 30 days, with a complete removal of the coach network by the end of the year.

My wife and I instantly felt all the emotions: Fear, self-doubt, anger, sadness, and everything in between. We poured our heart and soul into building our team, and they took it away. But there was nothing we could do. As coaches, we were all independent contractors, and they had complete control over ending our terms.

For 2 days, my wife and I felt like we were punched in the gut. We didn't sleep well. We felt nervous and scared. Our biggest concern became our livelihood and supporting our family. How will we survive? Our home? Our kids, etc.? My wife was distraught, understandably so, and insisted that she never again will join another multi-leveling marketing company. All the emotions of anger came out after having this stripped away from us.

But then it hit me after about 2 days of negative emotions. In the last 14 years, I have grown so much mentally that they can't take away from me what I learned, how I grew, and so much more. That is precisely what I share on stage when I speak. I cannot allow this loss to define us. We will figure it out and come out on top.

I then shared these exact words and affirmations on my social media. It said, "This time in my life will not define me. My history will not become my destiny. It may be a chapter in my life, but it's not the book of my life. I will have resolve. I will not be broken. You cannot take how I choose to respond. You don't know me. I am bigger than this. I am better than this. I will outwork this. I will grow to another level in my life. I will become even more. I will make an even bigger impact, I am one decision away and it starts with how I show up today. Today, I choose to win. Today, I choose to serve even more. Thank you, Beachbody, for the memories, but today is the day to take action on the new chapter of my life!"

We cannot control what happens to us, but we can control how we react. Without delay, within 2 days, I made the one decision to change my mindset quickly and swiftly. For one, I found gratitude in everything Beachbody has done for me and my family. The income, my health, the vacation trips, the lifelong friendships, and the business and life skills I developed. Furthermore, I wouldn't even be a keynote speaker if it wasn't for Beachbody. I found the gratitude that I made the one decision a few years back to retire and begin speaking, which has become my family's main income source. I had so much to be grateful for. I needed to flip the script in how I saw what happened to us.

WE CANNOT CONTROL WHAT HAPPENS TO US, BUT WE CAN CONTROL HOW WE REACT.

Then, more opportunities presented themselves. Two other super successful male leaders in Beachbody and I talked about teaming up and joining another company to form a super team – a dynasty of sorts. We never got to work together, but now we can build a bigger and new team and create something epic by bringing all of our people together. So, we began researching other opportunities in the health and wellness field and found something that we thought was even more powerful than where we were. Without delay, we all made the one decision and took action.

In a matter of days, we were part of a new company. My wife Kristen was even more excited than I'd seen her in a while, and we were focusing on the future. It was a whirlwind of a few days, and it still is today, but we were moving forward.

This is the epitome of the One Decision Away philosophy from every angle. At first, we faced every obstacle discussed above, leaving most people standing still – procrastination, loneliness, fear, comparison, holding onto the past, overcomplicating things, and more. We allowed ourselves to feel all the emotions but did not let them define us and hold us hostage. We immediately decided to move forward with a positive mindset and by taking actual physical action. We focused on many of the tools you will learn about in the upcoming chapters that drive decisions, such as your why, following your gut, and undeniable faith.

Last but not least, I hit pause on writing my book for a few weeks while I had to attend to launching our new business with a few keynotes sprinkled in as well. It's okay to make adjustments in our life when things like this come up. But what's not okay is doing nothing. Making no decision. We were committed to abiding by and understanding the One Decision Away philosophy 24/7/365. We recognized what we needed to do and immediately applied it.

I share this with you because we all face unexpected events like this in our lives. Maybe for some, it's a job loss. Maybe for others, it's facing the loss of a loved one. For some, it may be a sickness. But the One Decision Away philosophy can keep us going in times of uncertainty. It reminds us that obstacles and negative feelings are typical, but making *one decision* and moving forward is necessary. Nothing good comes out of standing still; it is not about making the perfect decision. It's about making a decision. At first, it started with deciding to find gratitude in everything that happened. Then, it was about making the one decision to move forward.

I am still experiencing many obstacles due to this change in my life, but the key is that I am committed to taking swift action backed by both courage and faith. In this case, the goal was to ensure my family was cared for. This could not happen without deciding to take action and move forward.

If you just experienced an unexpected life event, give yourself some grace, but do not sit still. My wife and I live by the 48-hour rule when the unexpected happens. We give ourselves 48 hours to go through all the emotions and process everything. Our 48-hour soap box if you will. But after that it's time to move forward and regroup. If you experienced an unexpected life event a few months ago and are still standing still, then it's time to move forward. Nothing good comes out of standing still. Is it easy to make the one decision to take the first step forward? No. Is it an absolute necessity for your healing and future success? Yes. 100 percent. It's time. Make the *one decision* and press forward.

3 *Key Takeaways*

1. Control How You Respond

You cannot always control what happens to you, but you can control how you react. Acknowledge your emotions, but don't let them define you. Adopt a new mindset from fear and loss to gratitude and opportunity – it's the first step toward moving forward.

ACTIONABLE EXERCISE

The next time you face a challenge, pause and write down your initial emotional reaction. Then, reframe it by listing at least three potential opportunities or lessons this situation could offer. Review your list and choose the most empowering perspective to focus on.

2. Take Swift Action

Obstacles will challenge you, but standing still is never the answer. Make one decisive action, even if it's small, to begin creating momentum. Action backed by courage and faith is the key to overcoming uncertainty and regaining control of your future.

ACTIONABLE EXERCISE

Pick one area of your life where you feel stuck. Write down one small, specific action you can take within the next 24 hours to create progress. For example, if it's a career obstacle, you might send an email or research a new opportunity. Commit to doing it immediately.

3. **Gratitude Opens Doors to Growth**

Finding gratitude in even the hardest circumstances can flip the script and create space for new opportunities. Reflect on what you've learned and how you've grown, then use that foundation to build the next chapter of your life.

ACTIONABLE EXERCISE

At the end of each day, write down three things you're grateful for — even if they seem small. For any challenges you faced that day, write one lesson or positive outcome you can take away. Use these reflections to start the next day with a growth-focused mindset.

CHAPTER 15

The Driving Force Behind the One Decision Away Philosophy

t was the day after my best friend David Brinkerhoff was shot and killed in the line of duty as a New York State Trooper. I was standing in his kitchen with his family and friends, and his wife, Barbara, approached me in front of their kitchen island and said, "David, I would like for you to do Dave's eulogy." With hesitation, I replied, "But Barb, why? He has two brothers. Why me?" She responded, "There is no one in the world I can think of who can honor and share Dave's life better than you." So I agreed and replied, "Of course. Ok."

The day had finally come to lay my best friend to rest. The church was packed with nothing but standing room for the funeral. The doors in the back were wide open so those standing outside and close enough could see inside. The streets were lined with thousands of police officers from around the world standing at attention. It was an impressive sight, but it's only one of those things you unfortunately see after a tragic event like this.

I was sitting in a pew on the right side of the church about halfway down. My mother was to my right, and my wife was to my left. I'll never forget when it was almost my turn to go up on the altar and speak. My mother put her left hand on my right leg and squeezed it just as I prepared to get up. An unspoken, powerful moment that needed no words. I know what my mom was saying.

I then went up on the altar, and in front of thousands of people, including a handful of dignitaries, such as people from the Governor's office, I shared and honored Brink's life. It was an extremely hard thing to do, but as I share this story with you today, I want to let you know I don't remember anything I said that day – not one word.

WHEN YOU HAVE A WHY IN YOUR LIFE, A DRIVING FORCE FOR WHY YOU DO WHAT YOU DO, YOU WILL DO THINGS YOU NEVER THOUGHT POSSIBLE.

However, this is what I learned that day: When you have a why in your life, a driving force for why you do what you do, you will do things you never thought possible. That day, he was my why. Today, my why is my wife and my three daughters, as well as all the people I can inspire when I speak, or people like you reading this book.

Remember, except for one tiny speck on this earth that makes up who you are, the world is composed of people other than you. It's about others each and every day. It's bigger than ourselves. People will not remember the car you drove or the house you lived in, but everyone will remember how you made them feel. When we learn to have a why bigger than ourselves and make it about others, not only will we be more apt to push through hard times, but we will also leave an impact on people we will never forget.

When it comes to making one decision, we often hesitate and don't take action because we are thinking of just ourselves. We must think bigger. We must focus from the inside out in life. It's about others. Our kids need the best of us. Our spouse or partner needs the best of us. Our co-workers need the best of us. The world needs the best of us. We have to get away from the selfish game and have a why that is bigger than ourselves.

I am not saying we shouldn't work hard for ourselves. It's okay to work hard to get new clothes, a new car, or a nicer home. We all need to strive to do that. Having nice things is far better than not. I am not denying that. But we must understand that in times of adversity, most people will quit because if it's just about them, they don't have a driving force to keep going. Conversely, no one wants to give up on something when it impacts someone else. People will work harder to avoid letting someone else down.

So, ask yourself, what is your why? If you don't have one, it's never too late to sit down, reflect for a few moments, and think about it. Ask yourself this one simple question. Who needs me on my "A" game today? Who needs me to be my very best today? Who needs me to show up today and get the job done no matter what happens? The answer to that is part of your why.

This should be a wake-up call for many of you because I feel too many people go through the motions in life. Whatever happens, happens. We throw in the towel and give up way too soon. That's because we have become so selfish in our ways that we often think the world revolves around us. Sometimes, it takes a wake-up call for us to realize it's not. I don't wish upon anyone that it takes sharing a eulogy for a loved one to understand the power of having a why, but maybe my story can help you find yours. When you find your why, you will always make the *one decision* each day to improve your life.

Every day I see my wife and my kids, and as I look into their eyes, I am reminded why I work so hard. I want to give them the best life possible. It's my duty and obligation to do this for them. Giving up or not trying is never an option. When it comes to the One Decision Away philosophy, every decision I make is driven by the power of having a why. It's not only a jumpstart to get you moving, but it should also continue as the inspiration to keep you going.

Remember this last tip. Your job and career are not more important than your family. As soon as I retired from the state police, as important as my position was, I was replaced with another captain immediately. My Beachbody business was stripped from me, and the entire community I was part of was taken away. We are not as important as we think we are. If your why is your family, don't work so hard you forget your loved ones because when you do retire, you may find yourself alone. Why? Because you never gave the ones you worked so hard for the light of day. That last email can wait. That last phone call can wait. The extra work project can wait. Spend time with your family. Don't miss all of your kid's sporting events. Don't miss all the school shows. Leave work a little early sometimes. Remember why you started. In summary, your why should be the driving force for the

One Decision Away philosophy, but you need to find a delicate balance to have a comfortable rhythmic balance in your overall life.

🔑 Key Takeaways

1. Your Why Is Your Driving Force

When your purpose is bigger than yourself, you'll find the strength to do things you never thought possible. Identify the people or causes that depend on you showing up as your best self every day. This clarity will push you forward, even in difficult times.

ACTIONABLE EXERCISE

Take 10 minutes to write down your "why" in detail. Include the names of the people or causes you're working for and how your actions impact them. Post this list somewhere you'll see it daily to remind yourself of the purpose behind your efforts.

2. Shift from Self-Centered to Service-Centered

Decisions rooted in service to others create lasting impact and purpose. Ask yourself daily, "Who needs me on my A-Game today?" Let this guide your actions and decisions to build a legacy that isn't about material possessions but about how you made others feel.

ACTIONABLE EXERCISE

Each morning, make a list of three people you can serve, support, or encourage that day. Then, follow through by sending a message, making a call, or taking a small action to help them. Reflect at the end of the day on how it made you feel.

3. **Balance Your Why with Presence**

While your why can inspire hard work, remember that the people you work for – your family, friends, and loved ones – need your presence more than your achievements. Prioritize time with them and never let your pursuit of success cause you to forget the ones who matter most.

ACTIONABLE EXERCISE

Schedule one "no distractions" hour each day to spend quality time with your loved ones. Put your phone away, turn off notifications, and focus on being fully present. On weekends, consider a whole day of just quality time for family, such as Sunday. Reflect weekly on how this time strengthens your relationships.

CHAPTER 16

Follow Your Gut

t's a phrase we all have heard at some point. Follow your gut, or the simple question: "What does your gut say?" It's not just some made-up phrase, but as a matter of fact, there is more behind the follow-your-gut intuition.

It's connected to something called your Enteric Nervous System (ENS). A "gut instinct" is often attributed to the activity of the ENS, a complex network of nerves located within the gastrointestinal tract that can send signals to the brain, essentially allowing the gut to "communicate" and influencing our emotions and decision making, sometimes leading to a feeling of intuition or a "gut feeling" when faced with a situation.

Disturbances in the gut, like stress or irritation, can trigger signals to the brain, leading to feelings of anxiety or discomfort, contributing to the "gut feeling" concept. However, due to its extensive neural network and ability to function somewhat independently, the ENS is often called the body's "second brain." It's not so little, either. The ENS is two thin layers of more than 100 million nerve cells lining your gastrointestinal tract from the esophagus to the rectum.

That is why you get butterflies in your stomach before a big game, presentation, or performance. Your ENS is actually activated, sending signals to your brain that create those butterfly feelings.

But I primarily want to talk to you about your gut instinct when it comes to growth areas of your life, such as going for that promotion, starting that new business, changing careers, trying out that new hobby, or asking someone out on a first date. The list goes on and on. More often than not, what you are actually feeling is a sign that you need to lean into that feeling and take action.

There is an epidemic of people who have a goal, dream, or vision for a better life but shy away from taking action because it makes them uncomfortable. However, they must embrace that feeling as a sign to make the *one decision* to move forward. Brendon Burchard calls this the "performance edge." It's that space we live in when we feel uncomfortable, knowing it's the right decision, but we shy away from it anyway.

NOTHING WORTH FIGHTING FOR IS COMFORTABLE.

Nothing worth fighting for is comfortable. We all have to be willing to go through a growth journey. We need to listen to our gut because in most cases, our gut instinct is correct. The pain of not trying later in life will far outweigh the pain of being uncomfortable and making that *one decision* to take the next step.

Every single benchmark I hit in life involved listening to my gut and battling through the butterflies. When I wanted to purchase a baseball batting cage at 12 years old, and my parents told me I needed to find a way to save the $3000 on my own, I knew in my gut that I needed to find a way. So, I decided to become a newspaper delivery boy, even though it would require a lot of hard work being outside during inclement weather.

When I wanted to become an ocean lifeguard, I was much smaller than most and wasn't the greatest swimmer. My gut said to "go for it," even though I was nervous about trying. What if I failed? What if I was not good enough? But I made the one decision and did it anyway.

When I was a New York State Trooper, I learned that the most challenging yearly award to receive was Trooper of the Year. It seemed like such a big undertaking, but my gut said to go for it, so I decided to do it. I accomplished that goal in 2003.

In 2010, when I was afforded the opportunity to build a direct sales multi-level marketing business to help me get out of debt, everyone immediately said it was a pyramid scheme. Don't do it. But again, my gut said, "Go for it." So, I leaned into my gut, made the decision, and built a million-dollar business.

When it came to retiring from the state police at 43 years old to pursue being a keynote motivational speaker, every-one called me crazy for leaving the state police and such a secure job. But my gut said, "You will regret this if you don't try," so I made the one decision and retired. Fast forward, and I have spoken to thousands of people around the country. Why? Because I followed my gut. I made the one decision.

The same thing happened when it came time to write my first book, *The Leveled Up Life*. I wasn't an english major or writer, but my gut said I had a message to share to help others. So, I leaned into it and published my first book. I made the one decision to follow my gut.

Right now, as I am training for an ultramarathon, I questioned whether I had the ability at 47 years old to accomplish such a task when I first started thinking about it a few months back. My gut said go for it. So, I followed my gut and made the decision. I am halfway through the training.

The point is that the uncomfortable butterfly "performance edge" you are experiencing is telling you something. You have two main ways to handle it. You can push those feelings away and not listen to them, or you can make the *one decision* to lean into them and go for it. I hate to tell you this, but if you decide to push those feelings away, at some point, you will start hearing the whispers again coming from your gut to take action. It's like a fire in your belly that you can't put out. You won't be able to stop that flame. You can't hide those feelings from your mind forever. They will always be there. The more times those gut instinctive feelings creep back into your mind, it will be an even stronger sign you need to make the *one decision* and follow your gut.

Your life is not about following your gut instinct just one time. The more you follow your gut to improve your life, the more times I believe God will put even more significant opportunities in your path. God will never give you something you can't handle. So, each time you are presented with some gut feelings, it is a sign from God telling you it's time to level up. You cannot sit still and expect great things to happen. You have to make one decision and take action! Life will reveal to you what's next. But you need to make the decision to start.

Here is the best part and what magically happens – something I have experienced firsthand. The more you follow your gut and decide to take action, the easier it will be to follow your gut the next time with what will likely be an even bigger decision. You will develop an even stronger mindset to lean into that next level of your life you are being called to pursue. You will develop the ability to get comfortable while being stretched and called to do something bigger and more impactful in your life. Making the decision to follow your gut will almost become automatic. You still will experience butterflies, but I can guarantee you will become bulletproof from procrastination and can sit there with a smile, knowing you are exactly where you are supposed to be. Let's go!

Remember, you miss 100 percent of the shots you are unwilling to take. That gut feeling was put there for a reason. It is telling you something. Don't push it away. I believe it was placed there by the creator. You need to make *one decision* and go after it. Suppose it doesn't work out. That's okay. Adapt and overcome. Keep pressing forward. Setbacks are part of the journey. You are not a failure. Setbacks are setting you up for the next level. Embrace the suck at times. Don't shy away. Make the one decision. Follow your gut. Onward and upward.

❸ Key Takeaways

1. Trust the Signals from Within

Your gut instinct isn't just a random feeling – it's a deep, inner signal rooted in your body's ENS, sometimes called your "second brain." This powerful network of nerves processes information and sends signals to your mind. When you feel those butterflies, discomfort, or an unshakable nudge, it's your body telling you something important. These moments of intuition are not obstacles to avoid but opportunities to embrace. Trust that these feelings are leading you toward growth and the next level of your life. Instead of pushing the discomfort away, recognize it as a call to action. Lean in, and remember: the discomfort you feel today is temporary, but the regret of not listening to your gut can last a lifetime.

ACTIONABLE EXERCISE

For the next week, keep a Gut Instinct Journal. Each time you feel a strong intuitive nudge — whether it's excitement, hesitation, or unease — write it down. Note the situation, what your gut is telling you, and whether you act on it. At the end of the week, review your notes and reflect on any patterns or insights that emerge.

2. Take Action, No Matter the Outcome

Making the one decision to follow your gut does not mean the path will always be easy or guarantee immediate success. Life is full of setbacks, challenges, and twists, but the real tragedy is doing nothing and staying stuck in your comfort zone. Even if you don't succeed on your first attempt, you'll gain valuable lessons and grow stronger for the next opportunity. Following your gut helps you build momentum, confidence, and resilience over time. Remember, the pain of trying and failing is far less than the pain of regret. Every action – whether it leads to success or a lesson – gets you one step closer to your ultimate goals and dreams.

ACTIONABLE EXERCISE

Identify one decision you've been overthinking and commit to taking action on it within the next 24 hours. It can be as simple as making a phone call, signing up for something new, or starting a project you've been delaying. No matter the outcome, reflect on what you learned and how you grew from taking action.

3. Build Confidence Through Repetition

Following your gut isn't a one-time event; it's a habit you can build. Each time you lean into those gut feelings and take action, you expand your comfort zone and strengthen your mindset. Over time, your confidence grows, and taking bold steps toward the unknown becomes second nature. What once felt intimidating will feel exciting, and the "butterflies" that used to scare you will now signal that you're exactly where you need to be. The magic is in the momentum — every decision to trust your instincts builds a foundation of self-belief, making it easier to pursue bigger and more impactful goals in the future.

ACTIONABLE EXERCISE

Create a Confidence Calendar. Each day for the next 30 days, take one small action outside your comfort zone — something that challenges you but aligns with your gut feelings. It could be speaking up in a meeting, introducing yourself to someone new, or trying something unfamiliar. Track your progress and celebrate each step forward.

CHAPTER 17

Your Best Teammate ... Faith

As we get older and wiser, we really come to learn what is truly important and what really matters. In our younger years, we often think we know everything and try to do everything alone. However, if there is one thing I wish I leaned more into as I navigated my 20s and 30s, it would be undeniable faith.

Faith is the belief in things you cannot see. At a certain point, we will feel completely lost about what to do next, and all we can rely on is faith. Nothing seems to be going right, and you are on the verge of calling it quits, but instead, you learn to lean into your faith.

For me, it's trust in God. I am not sure what your religious beliefs are, if any, and I am not saying you need to agree with mine, but I will say there is an immediate sense of peace and calm when you can learn

FAITH IS THE BELIEF IN THINGS YOU CANNOT SEE.

to have faith. Feel free to skip the rest of this chapter if you are not a person of faith or have any religious beliefs. But if you have faith, even if it's simply believing in a higher power such as the universe, feel free to keep reading.

I never just wanted to be average. I never just wanted to do just enough. You don't get rewarded in life for being average. No one recommends an average restaurant or average movie for you to go to. Life doesn't work that way. So why be an average human being? Unfortunately, the vast majority of people in this world go through the motions in life. They accept their life for what it is rather than lead their life to where they want to go. They never try to become more because it requires getting uncomfortable. If you are this type of person, you probably don't need to lean into faith too often because you are just going through the motions each day on your own. But I don't believe this is you because you wouldn't be reading this book if you were. Let me explain further for those trying to become more and go after their goals and dreams. There will come a time (for me it's almost daily) when you need to have massive faith. It will be a very lonely ride going after your goals and dreams. But you are not alone.

My daily goal is to do everything possible in my power to bring me closer to my goals. I refuse to be outworked. I will try new things. I will learn. I will grow. I will always give my best. This part is non-negotiable. Victim mentality, blaming others, or being lazy does not exist in my life. I do not operate this way with anything in my life. This first part is crucial because it leads into the second part, which is my secret to staying positive. I firmly believe that once I do everything in my power, I can surrender the outcome and the results to my faith in God. God, in my eyes, is my best teammate. Romans 8: 31-39 says, *"If God is for us, who can be against us?"* This is so powerful and meaningful to me. It allows me to surrender my life and the outcome of my life to him. With that comes an extreme sense of peace and calm in my life. If I do what I am supposed to, I know God will take care of the rest and never let me flounder. Now, if I was lazy or didn't do my job, this doesn't work. I am not asking God to cut me some slack and give me success I didn't earn, but I strongly believe when you do everything possible, there comes a point in time when you need to have faith that God will take care of the rest.

My friends, this has allowed me to take the leap of faith and make the decisions I have made so many times in my life. Leaving the state police was one of them, but even more, as I shared in Chapter 14, I had to surrender to God after we received the unexpected news that we were losing our business.

WHEN YOU DO EVERYTHING POSSIBLE, THERE COMES A POINT IN TIME WHEN YOU NEED TO HAVE FAITH THAT GOD WILL TAKE CARE OF THE REST.

All I had to go on was faith. When things seem bad you need to anchor your mindset on faith and make your decisions based on that. For me, it was having faith that my career as a speaker would continue to grow because God was on my side. Faith that our new business will grow because God is for us.

Looking back just 6 weeks, I can say with absolute certainty that this loss of our business happened for a reason. God needed to shed off some dead branches in our lives so we could grow even more. Even before we lost Beachbody, our business was slowly going downhill last year, negatively impacting my wife and me. This forced us to start a new business that my wife now loves and is excited about. Something she hasn't felt in a long time. It has also strengthened my faith that this journey as a motivational speaker is precisely where I need to be. God realigned the path of our life.

You are never alone. You are never in this by yourself. Yes, physically, you may be alone with no one there to support or cheer you on, but the most important person is. That is God. He is everywhere. Have faith in that.

When I first wake up, part of my morning routine is spending time in prayer, thanking God for what he has given me and asking for what I need. I wasn't always this way, and that is coming from someone who went to Catholic school his whole life. But at this stage in my life, I have come to accept and embrace the power of having faith in God; he is always by my side. When I go for a run, and the sun hits my face, I say thank you. When I see a beautiful sunset or sunrise, I take a moment to pause and feel grateful for God, who created this universe. I try to always live in a state of looking for signs and knowing God is right beside me. With that comes a powerful sense of what I call calm confidence.

It is an extremely lonely feeling right before I get on stage to speak. You look out into the crowd and know in a matter of seconds, all eyes will be on you. You are up there all by yourself with high expectations from your client to make an impact on the audience. I am sure there have been times when you needed to perform or present something and felt all alone. When this happens to me, I constantly repeat Philippians 4:13, *"I can do all things through Christ who strengthens me."* Within seconds, I am reminded that I am not alone because of my faith in God. He is beside me and will make sure I succeed.

In summary, as you navigate and apply the One Decision Away philosophy to your life, simply having faith keeps you moving forward to make those decisions. It's not going to be easy, and you will often still battle negative self-talk and worry, but do everything in your power to follow your gut and lean into faith. It's my secret weapon that anyone can activate in their life. Whatever you believe in, have faith that you are not alone. You are never alone.

③ *Key Takeaways*

1. Faith Provides Strength in Uncertainty

When faced with moments of doubt or fear, lean into your faith as a source of peace and guidance. Believing in something greater than yourself reminds you that you are not walking your path alone, even when the way forward seems unclear. When was the last time you felt uncertain about a decision? How could faith have helped you find peace in that moment?

ACTIONABLE EXERCISE

The next time you feel uncertain about a decision, pause for 5 minutes to reflect or pray. Focus on surrendering your doubts to your faith and ask for clarity or peace. Afterward, write down any thoughts or feelings that arise and take one small step toward resolving your uncertainty.

2. Faith Works Hand in Hand with Action

Faith is most powerful when paired with consistent effort. Take deliberate steps toward your goals every day, knowing that your hard work aligns with a higher purpose. Once you've done your part, let go of the worry and trust that your faith will guide the rest of the journey.

At the end of each day, write down one thing you accomplished to move closer to your goals and one way you trusted your faith to guide the outcome.

3. Faith Eliminates Loneliness on the Journey to Success

The pursuit of extraordinary goals can feel isolating, but faith reassures you that you are never truly alone. Trust that a higher power is guiding and supporting you, even when others don't see your vision. This belief creates a sense of calm confidence to keep moving forward, no matter what.

ACTIONABLE EXERCISE

Spend 5 minutes in silence today, reflecting on how faith has guided you in the past. Use this time to express gratitude for the ways a higher power has shown up for you and reaffirm your trust in that guidance moving forward.

CHAPTER 18

Focus on What's in Front of You

One of the most common things we often do as people is get so caught up in over-thinking everything we need to do. We think, and we think, and we think some more and wait for everything to be right before we start. Furthermore, we feel we need to figure out every single step before we take action and start moving closer to our goals. As mentioned in Chapter 12, this can be described as a paralysis of analysis. We are paralyzed from taking action on our life goals because all we do is analyze what needs to be done. We constantly consume so much information but fail to make the one decision to start. Instead of making the one decision, we ultimately make no decision and get caught in the hesitation trap. Far too many people end up living in this gap of hesitation.

Everyone's path to success will look different. We are all unique and different individuals. As of today, there are more than 8 billion people on this planet earth, and we are all uniquely different. So, wherever you are in your life, remember this one key detail to the success of your life. Work with what you have, with where you are, because what you have is plenty. I think that sentence is worth reading twice. Not only do you need to make the one decision to move forward, but you have more than enough areas of growth right in front of you that you can act on. You have plenty to work on. You need to focus on what's in front of you and not worry about how someone else does it. This is your life with its own unique sets of obstacles that you will face along the way. Start taking action on what's in front of you.

> **WORK WITH WHAT YOU HAVE, WITH WHERE YOU ARE, BECAUSE WHAT YOU HAVE IS PLENTY.**

You cannot want to "feel" like it to start. More often than not, you will not feel motivated to do the things you know you need to do. Feeling motivated is not going to be there most days. It's about understanding the principle of discipline and deciding to do it anyway. Here is the magical part about this. Once you start taking action, you will begin to feel motivated. It's the reverse of how we think this should happen. Most people think we need to first feel motivated to start, when in actuality, it's about starting, and then you will begin to feel motivated. Always remember, the ventral tegmental area of your brain will release dopamine. That's why motivation kicks in after you make the *one decision* to move forward. The more you do when you don't feel like doing it, the more motivated you will become each time you act. It's about taking action based on principles rather than our emotions. For example, I may not feel like writing this chapter of my book right now, but I know it needs to get done, so I do it no matter what. Then, as I get a couple of paragraphs in, momentum will kick in, and I'll start feeling motivated to do more and finish another chapter. Start stacking days of being disciplined no matter what. One day, then the next. Make the decision based on principles. Not your emotions.

Furthermore, as mentioned earlier, when you focus on making the one decision on what's in front of you, life will reveal to you what to do next. It is not the other way around. You do not need to have every step figured out before you start. Almost always, life is going to throw you obstacles, so your original plan will be thrown out the window anyway. It's about taking action, adapting, and overcoming. The one decision I made to talk to my wife many years ago, as mentioned earlier in the book, opened the door to everything else in my life, one step at a time. I focused on what was in front of me and made the one decision to take action and move forward. You cannot worry about anyone or anything else except what is in front of you.

There are about 2,800 billionaires in the world, and if you were to interview every single one, they would all describe different paths to becoming a billionaire. They may have some similarities regarding the field of work or investments they made. However, the obstacles they each faced along the way would all be different. Everyone's journey is their own, so stop copying what everyone else is doing. You are your own human being. Create and carve your own path. Be unique. If you want to live an exceptional life, you need to be willing to be the exception. You can't have one without the other. Your path will differ whether you want it to or not, so stop trying to be like someone else. Focus on yourself.

YOU ARE YOUR OWN HUMAN BEING. CREATE AND CARVE YOUR OWN PATH. BE UNIQUE.

Focus on your journey. Focus on what's in front of you and make the one decision to move forward.

Leadership expert and author John Maxwell said, "Once you find your why, you will find your way." As long as you know the driving force behind why you want to do something and why it's important to you, you will figure out the rest. You will find your way. In my own life, I never had all the answers. I'm not supposed to. But once I figured out why, I learned to focus on what was in front of me. Then everything else followed.

Navigating your own life and deciding to move forward is the great teacher of success. You often hear about lotto winners who win millions of dollars but end up right back where they were. How does this happen? How did they lose all that money? Quite simple. The person you become along the way as you learn how to earn a million dollars is far more valuable than the million dollars by itself. So stop looking for shortcuts. If a millionaire had their money stolen, they can earn it again because they developed the skillsets and mindset to become a millionaire. The lotto winner never developed any of this, so when they lost all their money, they ended up right back where they were. Focusing on what's in front of you allows you to grow and become the person you need to become to get to that next level.

I recently was on a Zoom call with a fellow speaker, and we talked about our upcoming goals for the following year and the strategies we need to use to get there. It was apparent that this fellow speaker's goals and plan of action didn't align.

They were focusing more on managing their current business rather than on the tasks needed to grow their business to the next level. I pointed this out, and they appreciated the tough love, but we are all guilty of this at some point. We don't want to make the one decision to take action on the often dull, monotonous, lonely tasks, but this is where the growth happens. It focuses on the actions we need to take right now, at this very moment in our own lives, to get to that next level.

As you finish reading this chapter, I want you to think about the one thing that you can do right now to improve your life or get closer to your goals. It doesn't matter how small it is. If you had to make one decision before you go to bed to move the needle, what would that be? Do you have the courage to take that step? It's a choice. Focus on what's in front of you and make that *one decision.*

③ Key Takeaways

1. Start Before You're Ready

Overthinking and waiting for the perfect moment often leads to inaction. You don't need to have every step figured out before you begin. The path forward will reveal itself as you move.

ACTIONABLE EXERCISE

Identify one area of your life where you've been stuck overanalyzing or procrastinating. Write down the very first step you can take today — no matter how small — and take action immediately. Momentum will follow once you begin.

2. Discipline Over Motivation

Motivation is unreliable — it won't always show up when you need it. Discipline, on the other hand, is built through consistent action, even when you don't feel like it. Action creates motivation, not the other way around. Remember, it's backed by science through the dopamine release from the ventral tegmental area of your brain.

ACTIONABLE EXERCISE

Commit to completing one task every day for the next 7 days that aligns with your goals — even if you don't feel like doing it. Track your progress and reflect on how you feel after completing each task.

3. Your Journey Is Unique

Stop comparing your progress or methods to others. Focus on your own path, obstacles, and strengths. Your journey is meant to be yours alone, and growth comes from working with what's in front of you.

ACTIONABLE EXERCISE

List three qualities or experiences that make your journey unique. Reflect on how these attributes can be leveraged to achieve your goals. Focus on using them as strengths rather than comparing yourself to others.

CHAPTER 19

Principles Over Emotions

one of us are immune to emotions. We all experience sadness, happiness, frustration, anger, joy, etc. We are all human; therefore, as emotional creatures, we all experience emotions all day. However, when it comes to reaching our goals and vastly improving our lives, I have learned that you should never make decisions when in an emotional state. It works at both ends of the spectrum. How often do you hear someone purchase something they can't afford because they were caught up in the excitement of having something? Maybe it was a car they couldn't afford or a piece of jewelry they couldn't afford, but they "loved it" so much that on the spot, they made the purchase only to regret it later. On the flip side, how often do you hear about someone in a state of anger or sadness doing something stupid that they usually regret for the rest of their life? Maybe it was quitting their goal, giving up on a dream they were pursuing, or even worse, committing a crime that may have even hurt someone. There are countless stories out there, but my main point is that we need to learn to make decisions based on principles, not emotions. I once heard motivational speaker Eric Thomas say, "At the end of our emotions is nothing. But at the end of every principle is a promise." In short, making decisions based on emotions alone often leads to a dead end, but if you follow life's principles, which are tried and true, you will frequently succeed.

When my wife and I were advised a few months ago that our Beachbody business was being shut down, we felt a lot of emotions going through our household. As mentioned in Chapter 14, we experienced anger, doubt, fear, frustration, and more. I distinctly remember when my wife was visibly upset with the news (to put it lightly) when we were discussing what just happened. She insisted we never get involved in a multi-level direct sales marketing business again. At the time, I agreed. We did not want to go through what happened ever again. We were passing blame, and truthfully, we let ourselves become the victims, which I am very against.

Victim mentality never gets you anywhere. But I remember saying we are going to follow our "48-hour rule," which means we get 48 hours to feel the way we are feeling, but after that, we need to brush ourselves off, refocus ourselves, and move forward based on the principles of life we live by. Being angry and playing the victim beyond 48 hours doesn't serve you. It's time to move on. We cannot let this setback define us. We choose how to react. Our company does not control our actions in the future. We do. We decide how to respond and what we will do next. We need to be open-minded and see what our options are. We had thousands of customers and hundreds of coaches from our team, so simply giving up was a selfish move. We have people we lead who look up to us, whether coaches on our team or one of our customers, so we need to pivot.

Additionally, our three daughters are watching, and we need to show them how to respond to life when they get knocked down. We began living our lives again based on principles. We made decisions based on what has proven to work: resiliency, no excuses, grit, a positive outlook, etc.

You must recognize when you are highly emotional and need to hit the pause button. This is one time in your life when it comes to applying the One Decision Away philosophy that you need to procrastinate a little to gather yourself and your emotions. Never make a decision when you are highly emotional. Here's a tip and something that works for me in the moment. I meditate a few times a week for a multitude of reasons. One main reason is my ability to calm myself down by slowing my breathing. When we are emotional, our bodies naturally respond by shortening our breaths and increasing our heart rate and blood pressure. It's a physiological response used as a defense mechanism that stems from the fight or flight syndrome to protect us. When you meditate, you learn to take long inhales and exhales over and over again. It both relaxes you and puts you in a state of calm. You cannot be irate and breathe slowly at the same time. It doesn't work. Now, here is the best part. When I get emotional, I can always catch my breath and immediately begin to slow my breathing by intentionally taking longer breaths. This slows my breathing, brings my heart rate down, and calms me down. This only happens because I practice meditation a few times a week. It's a secret that can work in many different environments whenever you are emotional. In the workplace, during tough conversations, when competing in a sporting event, etc. Anytime you feel yourself getting worked up, you can use this breathing method to calm yourself down. I like to inhale for 5 seconds and exhale for 10. Do this three times in a row, and you will feel refreshed and renewed. Remember, do not fall into the emotional trap. You need to recognize that your feelings can derail your process and often lead to impulsive decisions you may later regret.

You must develop consistent daily habits to create a pathway for success when emotions run high. I will never stop talking about the power of daily exercise and how it translates to how you show up and handle everyday life. Getting yourself dressed and out the door to exercise requires discipline, and the more consistent you are, the more disciplined you become. Furthermore, pushing yourself through a hard workout develops perseverance, grit, and determination to finish. These are all attributes that we can use to succeed in everyday life. Because I exercise 6 days a week and have developed everything mentioned above, I have pushed through the hard times in my life. When I lost my Beachbody business, I could adjust and press forward because I have developed perseverance and other positive attributes and principles that always take me down the right path. The same goes for reading personal development books. The more you learn and expand the capacity of your mind, the better you become at handling life. Something that once seemed impossible now becomes easy because you have grown as an individual. Incorporating daily behaviors such as exercise and reading will positively impact your life, especially when you become emotional.

Perseverance is my superpower. Nothing is more important to me than never giving up, no matter what. Too often, when things get hard, we quit and are quick to pass blame. We become emotional and give up. However, your future is determined by the choices and decisions you make. No one is coming to save you. If you are going to succeed, it is on you; therefore, giving up is never an option. You must persevere.

As mentioned previously, in 2023, when I ran the New York City Marathon, my body completely broke down with major cramps in both my legs, my right arm, and also the right side of my back. As much as I initially planned to strive for a personal record that day, my goal changed from hitting that PR to simply finishing, which I did in 4½ hours. I was in tears of pain, but giving up was never an option. Too often, we give ourselves a Plan B. I am not a fan of Plan B's because you are already giving yourself a way out. Plan B, for me, is never an option. I once read that Navy Seals make up in their mind before they set out on a mission that they are going to complete that mission. It doesn't matter if they get shot or hurt; the only thing they care about is completing the mission. They don't have a Plan B. They are the epitome of perseverance and make their decisions based on the principle of perseverance rather than their emotions of pain.

What are the core values in your life? My core values are more important than making decisions based on my feelings. Living a principle-driven life following your core values will lead to great success. Both externally by what you accomplish in the outside world and internally by how you feel about yourself. For me, I strive each day to do what's right. Don't take shortcuts in your life. Don't cheat. Do the right thing. Have patience. If it's too good

LIVING A PRINCIPLE-DRIVEN LIFE FOLLOWING YOUR CORE VALUES WILL LEAD TO GREAT SUCCESS.

to be true, it probably is. Hang around good people. Always be teachable and coachable.

Strive to live a life with integrity, commitment, and purpose. You need to put your head on the pillow at night, and I could never live with myself if I didn't live a life with integrity. Often, doing the right thing isn't the easy thing. But you can always live with yourself when you have integrity and never have to worry about it returning to haunt you.

Additionally, stay committed to what you started, which means sticking to what you said you would do when you face opposition. When you are only interested in something, you do it when you feel like doing it. When you are committed to something, you do it no matter what. So always be committed.

Lastly, live your life with purpose. It should always be for something bigger than yourself. When you put people first and lead with a servant mindset, it will come back to you repeatedly. Both mentally and financially. Zig Ziglar once said, "Help enough people get what they want, and you will get what you want." When I speak, I always ask God before I get on stage, "God, please put the words in my mouth you need me to speak and connect me to those you need me to meet." I want to focus on other people and impact their lives for the better. My goal each day is to positively impact one person in their life so their life can get better. It drives me and gives me purpose and meaning to what I do. The same goes for this book. This allows me to reach people I will never meet so that maybe they can apply the One Decision Away philosophy to their lives. Live with purpose. Focus on others.

I also always remind myself that God is always watching. I am never alone. That extra good deed you took action on, he sees you. But also, he saw the shortcut or small lie you shared. This keeps me on the right path each day to always focus on doing the right thing. Whether you are emotional or not going about your day, always focus on your core values. Make your decisions based on principles, not on your emotions. Take it one day at a time. *One decision* at a time. If you can do this, you will be in a much better place throughout your life.

> **MAKE YOUR DECISIONS BASED ON PRINCIPLES, NOT ON YOUR EMOTIONS.**

❸ Key Takeaways

1. Decisions Based on Emotions Often Lead to Regret

Emotions are a natural part of life, but making impulsive decisions when emotional – whether in excitement, anger, fear, or sadness – often results in regret. Principles, not emotions, should guide your decisions because principles lead to long-term success and fulfillment.

ACTIONABLE EXERCISE

Think about a past decision you made in an emotional state that you later regretted. Write down what emotions influenced that decision and how you would approach it differently using principles instead. Next time you feel overwhelmed by emotions, remind yourself to pause before deciding.

2. Create Systems to Ground Yourself in Principles

When emotions run high, having established habits – such as the 48-hour rule or daily meditation – helps you regain clarity before making decisions. Consistent habits like exercise, reading, and breathing techniques train your mind to act based on principles rather than temporary emotions.

Choose one grounding practice to implement in your daily routine (e.g., meditation, journaling, or exercise). The next time you feel emotionally charged, use that practice to pause and center yourself before taking action.

3. Commit to Living with Integrity, Commitment, and Purpose

Making principle-driven decisions means always doing the right thing, staying committed even when things get tough, and focusing on a purpose bigger than yourself. Success comes when you align your actions with your core values, not fleeting emotions.

ACTIONABLE EXERCISE

Write down three core values that will guide your decision-making. When faced with a challenging situation, check if your choice aligns with these values. If it doesn't, reassess before taking action.

CHAPTER 20

Be the Best Version of You

You cannot burn the candle at both ends of your life and expect to succeed at the highest level. I have been here myself too often in my life. It got so bad that I found myself once dry heaving in the bathroom from stress. I'll talk about that in more detail, but first, I want you to understand that I know what it's like to struggle daily. I know what it's like to feel stressed and overwhelmed sometimes. I know what it's like to feel like you barely have enough time to eat and go to the bathroom, nonetheless find time to exercise and do other things to take care of ourselves (who has time for that, right?!). I understand.

I am married and have three daughters, and as far back as I can remember, I always had to do additional work to either help support myself in my younger years when my parents were going through a divorce or to support my family. It is easy to blame others, your circumstances, where you live, lack of support, etc. Playing the victim card is easy, and quite frankly, that's how the vast majority of society lives. We blame others and want to blame everyone else for our failure. But I also know this: Until you accept complete responsibility for your life and take ownership of your actions, you will never achieve the life you want to live. I can say this now because of what I went through and where I am today. I recognize all of the personal growth it took to get here. You cannot be the best version of yourself if you are in constant survival mode each day.

UNTIL YOU ACCEPT COMPLETE RESPONSIBILITY FOR YOUR LIFE AND TAKE OWNERSHIP OF YOUR ACTIONS, YOU WILL NEVER ACHIEVE THE LIFE YOU WANT TO LIVE.

I will never forget this day. My wife was across the country attending a conference for our business, so I took care of my three little daughters by myself when she was away. At the same time, I was recently promoted to captain with the New York State Police and had started taking on some of my new responsibilities before my first official day. I was also training the incoming lieutenant who was replacing me. My role at the time was overlooking multiple high-level undercover units that covered New York City, such as organized crime, auto theft, money laundering, large-scale drug operations, labor & racketeering, and more. It was a busy place. Simultaneously, our Beachbody direct sales business was not doing well, causing a lot more stress on my wife and me. While all this was happening, I was in my office, and the phone rang. It was my middle daughter's elementary school, and they thought my daughter had broken her wrist. They needed me to come to school to pick her up to take her to the hospital.

That night, I was sitting on the couch, completely overwhelmed and stressed. I found myself in the bathroom minutes later, dry heaving from stress. It was the worst feeling of my life. I wasn't having suicidal thoughts, but I knew I needed help. There was too much all at once, and I could barely keep up. What happened next changed my life. I drummed up the courage to pick up the phone and ask for help – something very hard for a police officer. We have been trained or at least trained to be perceived as bulletproof when dealing with stress, especially with all that we encounter, see, and deal with. But I also knew far too many police officers commit suicide. On the inside, many police officers struggle. It is a daunting and taxing job on your mental well-being.

I got the name of a local therapist, picked the phone up, and called her. The decision to do that completely changed my life. Having someone to tell me what I was feeling was completely normal and that I was not "nuts." However, I understood that if I didn't take control of my life and take care of myself first, I would end up having a complete breakdown. This was when I was first introduced to the concept that you need to be willing to put yourself first. If you don't take care of yourself first, then everyone gets what's left of you, not the best of you. I am a disservice to my wife, my kids, and the people I serve by showing up in a mental state like that. Taking care of my physical and psychological well-being was selfless, not selfish.

I openly admit I shed some tears with my wife and promised her that I would work as hard as I did on myself as I did in all the other areas of my life. By this point, I had achieved high earnings with our business, moved up through the ranks of the state police, led many people within the state police and our business, and also made sure to be there for my family daily.

IF YOU DON'T TAKE CARE OF YOURSELF FIRST, THEN EVERYONE GETS WHAT'S LEFT OF YOU, NOT THE BEST OF YOU.

I always had a strong work ethic, but now it was time to put that effort into improving myself. The first book I was introduced to read was *The Four Agreements* by Don Miguel Ruiz. I ordered it on Audible and finished it within about 2 days. It was eye-opening. The second thing I was told to start incorporating was meditation. As much as I felt up until this point that this was some hokey pokey type of activity, I was willing to try because of my mental state. This, too, was life-changing. I learned to calm down my mind and handle stress throughout the day better.

I also learned to practice gratitude daily and begin each day by writing down things I am thankful for. No matter how simple they were, such as food in my fridge, I intentionally found gratitude for whatever I had. Far too often, we focus on what we don't have instead of on what we do have. It was a flip of my mindset.

The activities I learned to practice through therapy were eye-opening. They shifted how I felt about the world and myself, but the biggest takeaway was the importance of scheduling time for yourself, like a doctor's appointment I couldn't miss. When something becomes a priority for you,

you will always find a way to get it done. Otherwise, you will find an excuse.

Did I have to make sacrifices to ensure I practiced all my new activities? Yes, I did. But it was more about cutting out things that no longer served me. For example, staying up late, scrolling social media, and watching television did not serve me, so I drastically reduced my time spent on them.

My morning routine to this day has become sacred to me. I choose to get up before everyone else in my house does. There is something about sitting downstairs in my home when most of the world is still asleep, my phone isn't going off, and emails aren't coming in, where I can focus on my gratitude for the day, meditate, and pray. While doing this, I am either sipping a morning cup of coffee or my pre-workout drink because in less than an hour, 6 days a week, I get in my exercise and workout. Remember, exercise doesn't cost you time. It buys you time back because you will be more efficient, less stressed, and get more done each day in the same amount of time. After all, you take care of your body, and it will take care of you. You can't afford not to exercise multiple days a week.

Working on my mindset first, followed by some daily exercise, creates a tremendous sense of accomplishment and fulfillment while being ready to tackle the day with whatever life throws at you. It's that dopamine release again from the ventral tegmental area of your brain that creates momentum for the rest of the day. You are coming from a place operating at a much higher mental state. Too many people wake up and are immediately in reactive mode. You are checking your phone notifications (by the way, I like to say your notifications on your phone are someone else's agenda), getting your kids ready for school, and getting yourselves ready at the same time. Then we rush out the door, trying to get to work on time. This is not a way to live or be the best version of yourself. I get up before all this craziness starts so I can take care of myself first. The power of a morning routine is worth its weight in gold. People will say they aren't a morning person. No one is. Who wants to get out of a warm bed? No one! You must create that version of yourself by deciding to start. The more you do it, the easier it gets. Again, if it's a priority, you will find a way.

Why do I share all this? To be the best version of yourself and thus be able to act on things to live a more extraordinary life, it starts with getting yourself out of "survival mode." For many, this may mean simply putting yourself first, as I did. You must go through your growth journey to get your mind right. Maybe the one decision you need to make today is getting professional help, too. Perhaps it's to stop watching Netflix every night and do something that will serve you positively instead. i.e., exercise.

What is the cost to your future self by not caring for yourself now? What is the cost to your future self by not at least trying? Do you want to live in a state of survival each day? Do you want to live each day on repeat? Or would you rather have a day full of great energy, be excited about your future, feel happy, and simply slay life? We only get one shot at this thing called life, and for you to be the best version of yourself, you need to be operating from a level of excellence each day. You need to be operating from a higher state and have a little bounce in your steps and a smile on your face.

WHAT IS THE COST TO YOUR FUTURE SELF BY NOT CARING FOR YOURSELF NOW?

Whatever it is that you decide to do, give it your all. Be your best. Don't give it 50 percent. Too many people are stuck in third gear and have so much more left in them. You were placed on this earth for a reason. The chances of becoming a human are 1 in 400 trillion. Do not waste it.

No matter what trials and tribulations you have been through until now, no matter what challenges you have faced throughout your life, today is a new day, and you are *one decision away* from having that vision again. *One decision away* from changing your mindset for the better. *One decision away* from stopping procrastination in your life. *One decision away* from putting yourself on the path to becoming the best version of yourself. You need to always strive to be the best version of yourself.

❸ Key Takeaways

1. Prioritizing Yourself Is Selfless, Not Selfish

Taking care of yourself is not an act of selfishness – it's an act of responsibility. When you neglect your physical and mental well-being, you are doing a disservice to yourself and those who rely on you. Operating from a place of stress, exhaustion, or survival mode limits your ability to lead, support, and serve at your highest potential. You cannot pour from an empty cup.

ACTIONABLE EXERCISE

Create a "Non-Negotiable Self-Care List." Write down three things you will commit to doing daily or weekly to prioritize yourself. This could be 30 minutes of exercise, reading for personal growth, or setting boundaries around work hours. Then, schedule these into your calendar as if they were an unmissable doctor's appointment. The goal is to make self-care a routine, not an afterthought.

2. Your Daily Routine Determines Your Future

Your success and well-being are the result of your daily habits. The way you start your day sets the tone for everything that follows. A chaotic, reactive morning leads to a scattered, unproductive day, while an intentional morning routine builds momentum, energy, and focus. You don't need hours – you need discipline and consistency.

Design a "Power Hour" Morning Routine. If you don't already have a structured morning routine, start with just 30-60 minutes of intentional activities. Choose at least three of the following:

- Gratitude practice (write down three things you're thankful for)
- Meditation or deep breathing (5-10 minutes to calm your mind)
- Exercise (even 20 minutes of movement will make a difference)
- Journaling or affirmations (to set your mindset for the day)
- Reading or listening to personal growth content

Commit to this for 7 days straight, track how you feel, and adjust as needed. Over time, this routine will become a non-negotiable part of your day.

3. You Are One Decision Away from Change

No matter how long you've been stuck in a pattern, change happens the moment you decide to take action. You don't need to wait for motivation or the perfect moment – the power to change is already in your hands. The key is making one small, intentional decision today that moves you forward.

ACTIONABLE EXERCISE

Identify one decision you've been avoiding and take action on it today. Ask yourself:

- What is one area of my life where I've been procrastinating change?
- What's one small decision I can make right now to move forward?

Examples:

- If you've been neglecting your health, schedule a workout today.
- If you've been overwhelmed at work, delegate or ask for support.
- If you've been feeling stuck mentally, book a therapy or coaching session.

Write down your one decision and take action within the next 24 hours. Momentum builds from the first step!

CHAPTER 21

Trust the Process

We live in a time where we can get any information at our fingertips in seconds. Our cell phones today are significantly more powerful than the computer used to land on the moon during the Apollo 11 mission in 1969. They have 100,000 times more processing power than the Apollo Guidance Computer. It's absolutely insane the power we have at our fingertips through our cell phones. Furthermore, when we buy something online, it's at our house in a matter of days. Amazon Prime orders now arrive within 2 days, sometimes even on the same day! Did you know you can now order a tiny home on Amazon and receive it within a week?! Seriously, go check it out. It's unbelievable! Unfortunately, success in life doesn't work this way. The problem, however, is we have become so accustomed to getting anything and everything we want, right now. But when it comes to achieving our goals in life, there is no overnight shipping. Everything takes time. A lot of time. More often than not, it will take ten times longer than we ever expected. We will face unforeseen obstacles. We will need to adjust our plans. We will need to grow and learn new things along the way. It will be beyond challenging. But here is the positive news. If you are willing to understand that when you make the *one decision* to improve your life, no matter the goal, and trust the process, you will be way ahead of the game. You will be setting yourself up for success. Accepting this will put you ahead of most people because most want results right now! Life doesn't work that way.

Whenever I set my mind to do something, it always costs more time and energy than anticipated. I am more patient today, so I have learned to double the timeframe and anticipate twice as many problems from my initial thoughts. I'll never forget when my keynote speaking coach told me that building this business is a solid 2-4 year build. I wasn't expecting to hear that, and for a while, it was very unsettling because no one wants to work so hard for at least 2 years with minimal return. I was shocked. But as I entered year 4 of being a professional speaker, my coach was 100 percent right. I quickly learned that even if someone likes you as a speaker, more often than not, they already have their speakers booked for that year. So then you could be waiting at least 1-2 years for that event to get back to you. Your hard work takes a long time to return to you. Not only is this line of work very competitive, but you must also endure the waiting game and have extreme patience. Your goals are going to take time. There is not a single super successful person out there with a solid foundation under them who did it overnight. Most of what you see on social media is a facade, and yes, there may be a few one-hit wonders, but the most successful people implore macro patience. They spent years working hard when no one was watching and nobody knew them. Getting in shape and working out at the gym is one of the best level playing fields because there is no shortcut to getting fit and strong. It takes time, effort, consistency, and discipline. You absolutely must trust the process. There are no shortcuts. Be patient.

There will be days when you don't feel like doing it, especially when you have worked so hard for so long. Be kind to yourself and understand this is part of the process. However, we must remember we are the sum total of one simple daily decision. That is, whether we choose progress or choose to live with our excuses. You can't have both, and the longer you choose excuses, the further away progress becomes. It's a choice. Don't allow your excuses to get the best of you. Make the *one decision*, keep going, and trust the process.

WE ARE THE SUM TOTAL OF ONE SIMPLE DAILY DECISION. WHETHER WE CHOOSE PROGRESS OR CHOOSE TO LIVE WITH OUR EXCUSES.

Whenever you embark on a new journey, remember this: Do not ever take advice or criticism from someone less successful than you or who has never accomplished what you are trying to achieve. We far too often let the negative comments from the haters and critics rent space in our heads that frequently derail us from our goals. Especially from those who have never walked in your shoes or have accomplished anything worthwhile to talk about! Let them go! Do not let them stop you from achieving your goals! We let one negative social media comment stop us far too often. There could be

100 positive comments, but that one will get you every time. Our job is not to please everyone. Our job is to live our best life possible. It's your life. Not theirs.

To stay patient and endure the obstacles that will come your way, you must love what you do. If you don't love it, then you will never make it. There is no way around it. When times get tough, the only thing that keeps us going is our love for what we do. No miserable person will push through difficult times if they hate it. That's almost the definition of insanity. Torturing yourself and facing problems doing something you hate is a miserable place to live. On the flip side, when you find something you love to do, you have identified the secret to what it takes to succeed and win: love.

I love running, and that's how I made it through ultramarathon training. I love to speak to serve and empower others, and that's what keeps me motivated if someone else gets chosen over me to speak at an event. I love the feeling of a sense of fulfillment and accomplishment. That's why I am always setting big new goals. You must love it so you can keep going. If you are in a job or career you absolutely hate, as scary as this can be, you need to change what you are doing; otherwise, you will feel very unfulfilled and set yourself up to feel miserable. You cannot get time back. You may need to cut the security rope of what you are currently doing so you can live the life you were meant to live.

Last but not least, as you learn to trust the process, remember complaining gets you nowhere. How you choose to respond is a choice. Your attitude is a choice. No one wants to be around someone with a poor attitude. It's exhausting and draining. Your attitude in life will determine your altitude. You cannot succeed if you are in a constant state of being negative and complaining all the time. Also, maybe you need to hear this, but no one cares about your problems. I know that may hurt, but it's the truth. We all have our problems to deal with, and no one cares about ours. We all get knocked down. We all get stressed. We are all busy. You are not the victim. How you choose to respond separates the winners from the losers. Choose to respond with a positive attitude. Make that *one decision*!

We all must trust the process every day. Don't worry about what will come tomorrow; rather, make the one decision and give it your very best today. The more consistent you

YOUR ATTITUDE IN LIFE WILL DETERMINE YOUR ALTITUDE.

are each day, the further the compound effect will kick in and benefit you tomorrow. It's about who you become during the journey. Take it one day at a time. One decision at a time.

❸ Key Takeaways

1. Success Takes Time — Trust the Process

In a world of instant gratification, real success doesn't happen overnight. The biggest goals take time, patience, and perseverance. Expect the journey to take longer than anticipated, and embrace the challenges along the way.

ACTIONABLE EXERCISE

- Write down a big goal you're working toward.
- Now, double the timeframe you originally expected to achieve it. Accept that obstacles will come and that persistence is key.
- Each day, write one small action step you took toward that goal. Over time, these small steps will compound into big results.

2. Block Out the Noise and Stay Focused

Never take criticism from someone who hasn't done what you're trying to achieve. Most people let negative comments, fear of judgment, or temporary setbacks derail them, but those who succeed stay locked in on their purpose.

ACTIONABLE EXERCISE

- Identify one negative opinion or self-doubt that has held you back.

- Ask yourself: Is this coming from someone who has achieved what I want? If not, dismiss it.
- Instead, seek out one mentor, book, or podcast from someone who has succeeded in your field and study their approach.

3. Your Attitude Determines Your Altitude

How you respond to setbacks, obstacles, and daily struggles will determine your success. Complaining solves nothing – adjusting, learning, and taking action does. Your attitude is a choice. Trust the process. Stay patient. Stay focused. Take action. Every day, you are one decision away from moving forward. Keep going!

ACTIONABLE EXERCISE

- The next time you catch yourself complaining, immediately reframe it into an action.
- Example: Instead of "I don't have time to work out," say, "I will schedule a 15-minute session today."
- Make this a habit: Every night, write down one challenge from your day and how you responded to it. Over time, train yourself to always choose action over excuses.

CHAPTER 22

Your Excuses Are Exhausting

here is nothing that is going to hold you back from actually taking action on the one decision you know you need to make other than excuses. We use excuses so often in our lives that it gets to the point that we start believing them as truths. We become too blind to recognize the excuses we tell ourselves. At the end of the day, our success has nothing to do with our circumstances. But everything has to do with the excuses we tell ourselves. Excuses become exhausting to hear, and they are everywhere. I'm at the point in my life that when I listen to someone make excuses, I just sit there and entertain myself internally, pointing out in my head all the excuses they are making. I once heard Dani Johnson say, "Excuses are well-planned lies." Ouch, but so true.

Average people make excuses. Average people play victim mentality. But the greats talk about solutions. The greats play victor mentality, not victim mentality. Those that are

THE GREATS PLAY VICTOR MENTALITY, NOT VICTIM MENTALITY.

successful go about their day in a different way. An uncommon way but that's why they are so successful.

Why do we make excuses? Ultimately to make ourselves feel good in one of two ways. We use them to make peace with ourselves or so we can think that someone else will understand and agree with our excuse so they don't look at us negatively. Making excuses shifts responsibility away from ourselves and instead passes the blame onto someone or something else. It is a way that we try to make ourselves feel good by failing to take ownership of our lives.

I have no time for excuses. Have I been guilty of making some at times? Of course, absolutely. We all do. But I didn't get to where I am today by making excuses. I got here by overcoming whatever nonsense I told myself and instead put in the work.

We need to avoid living in the gap of hesitation that often arises right before we start to do something. We experience the hesitation to start, the hesitation to get up on time, the hesitation to have the tough conversation, the hesitation to start exercising, the hesitation to start the dream business, etc. Far too many people live in this gap of hesitation, and the main reason why is that we allow excuses to start creeping into our minds, eventually stopping us from taking action. The more excuses you have, the harder it will be to overcome them because your mind is like a muscle. What you feed your mind expands and grows. Feed your mind with excuses and the excuses that let you not do something become prevalent. The key is to self-audit yourself and recognize your excuses. Excuses are often fear, doubt, and laziness disguised as reasoning that keeps us in our comfort zones. However, nothing worthwhile happens in our comfort zones, so we must be able to rid ourselves of our excuses.

Here are some of the most common excuses we often hear and probably have all been guilty of at one time or another. First, one of the most common excuses we hear justified is lack of time. "I am just too busy." The fact is everyone is busy. You are not the only one with a hectic life. But those who are successful in their life, despite being busy, have found a way to manage their time more effectively. It's not that you don't have time. We all have the same 24 hours in the day. If it's not your priority, you make the excuse of time. Stop saying you are too busy. Instead, say it's not a priority for me right now.

The excuse of being too old to do something is another. There are countless stories of people achieving unbelievable success in their later years. As mentioned earlier my friend Joe Gagnon, an ultramarathoner and author of *Living the High Performance Life*, didn't start running until the age of 40, where he could barely complete a mile! To date, he has logged over 55,000 miles running, and 135,000 miles biking, completed 6 Ironman triathlons, over 60 ultramarathons, 35 marathons, and even completed a "Six Continent Challenge" – a marathon a day for 6 days on 6 continents. Furthermore, Colonel Harland Sanders was a failure by most conventional standards for much of his life. After trying multiple careers, including as a farmer, steamboat pilot, and gas station owner, he finally perfected his fried chicken recipe in his 60s. Sanders traveled door-to-door to pitch his chicken recipe to restaurants, facing rejection after rejection. At 62, he founded Kentucky Fried Chicken, and the brand eventually grew into one of the most recognized franchises in the world. Ray Kroc was a struggling milkshake machine salesman when he stumbled upon a small hamburger stand run by the McDonald brothers. At 52, Kroc saw its potential, partnered with the brothers, and transformed it into the McDonald's we know today. By standardizing operations and focusing on scalability, Kroc built the largest fast-food franchise in the world. Need I say more? Don't use age as an excuse. If you have a heartbeat and air in your lungs, it's never too late to make the decision to pursue your goals and dreams.

I am too tired is just another excuse. People who are too tired are often the product of poor sleep habits, improper nutrition, and lack of exercise. Deciding whether to go to bed at 10 p.m. or stay up to midnight watching Netflix is a choice. Deciding whether to pack a healthy lunch for work or order something most likely unhealthy is a choice. Deciding whether to scroll social media for hours a day or replace it with 30 minutes of exercise daily is a choice. If appropriately acted upon, all of these decisions lead to more energy, less stress, and better sleep. Too tired is a choice.

Talent alone will never lead to success. There are countless stories of less talented people willing to outwork their competition and win. Too many talented people are lazy and take their gifts for granted. I wake up every single day with the same thing in mind. You may be a better speaker than me. You may be a better runner. You may be a better writer. You may be a better businessman, but you will not outwork me. I will beat you every single day of the week when it comes to work ethic and hustle. That's the standard I have set for myself. We too often blame our lack of talent for lack of success. It's an excuse. Outwork your competition.

Another excuse you could be telling yourself is that you don't have enough money to go to conferences, hire coaches, or take courses. Again, lack of money is an excuse. There are countless free ways to learn almost anything on the internet. I have watched thousands of hours of other motivational speakers on YouTube for free. Not only did it help me grow my mind, but I also picked up so many golden nuggets about my style of delivery on stage. You can find anything you need to know by simply typing G-O-O-G-L-E. It's free. Don't use lack of money as a reason why you can't do something. Again, it's an excuse.

After suddenly losing my best friend, I live by the motto "life doesn't always fire a warning shot." We far too often talk about doing things when we have more time or are less busy or maybe next week. But I like to say we may not be here tomorrow. It's what we do with today that matters. Every single day is a blessing and gift. Tomorrow is not guaranteed. It's what you do with the today that matters.

News flash! People will not support you in your quest to improve your life, and more often than not, the ones closest to you will be your harshest critics, i.e., family. So don't let the excuse of not having support stop you from making the *one decision* to commit to your goals and dreams. Success doesn't rely on others. It relies on you taking ownership of your life and going after your goals and dreams. It is no one else's job to support your goals and dreams other than yourself. I had next to no support in building my direct sales business, writing my first book, and becoming a speaker. But I learned to accept that other people's opinions of me are not my reality. Their opinions of me are none of my business. It is my life. Not theirs. The next time you complain about lack of support, remember it's simply an excuse.

Struggle is less painful than regret, therefore the worst thing you want is a life where you look back and wish you had done something. We cannot get time back. One of the driving forces for me to retire from the state police at 43 years old was the fear of looking back at my life and saying to myself, "What if I actually succeeded in being a paid professional motivational speaker? I wish I tried." That fear of regret drove me to make the one decision to take action. Each day that goes by, when you put something off that you know you need to do, success evades you. Do not live with regret.

When I was a senior in college with 12 credits left to graduate with my bachelor's degree, I decided to leave college to enter the New York State Police Academy. I could have easily allowed excuses to get in my way, but in my heart, that was the only career and job I ever wanted. I loved everything about what I could do as a police officer, so I took that leap of faith. I am so grateful and glad that I did because it was the most fun, rewarding, and fantastic career, and I met some of the best people. I got to work with one of the best law enforcement agencies in the world. I miss the people every single day. I could have easily turned down this opportunity because of excuses, but instead, I made the one decision to lean into my calling when it came to me.

As you go throughout your day, I want you to try to recognize all the things you do that aren't serving you. Those things that open the door to your excuses. For example, what is the screen usage on your phone? Could that time be used more wisely, working on things that will improve your life? Would the excuse of being too busy or too tired finally look silly? What about watching television? Or steaming shows on your iPad? How much time do you waste on that?

When it comes to keeping life simple and living a one decision away life, you must recognize that your excuses delay decisions. But when you learn to overcome them, you move closer to success. The more you overcome your excuses, the easier life becomes. It starts with the decisions you make today.

I have a challenge for you. I want you to try to live an "Excuse Free Week." For one week, every time you find yourself making an excuse, write it down and course correct. Immediately. Without delay. Keeping track will help you see how often you are hindering yourself from success, and correcting your course in the moment will move you closer to your goals. Like I said above. Keep it simple. Your success is *one decision away*, but your excuses keep you on the wrong side of that decision.

❸ Key Takeaways

1. Excuses Are Justifications for Inaction

Excuses are a way to shift responsibility away from ourselves, keeping us comfortable but stagnant. The more we repeat an excuse, the more we start believing it as truth. However, success is built on ownership, not excuses. Recognizing your excuses is the first step to eliminating them.

ACTIONABLE EXERCISE

For the next 3 days, write down every excuse you catch yourself making — no matter how small. At the end of each day, review your list and ask: is this really true, or am I just avoiding responsibility? Next, replace each excuse with an action step. Example: instead of "I'm too tired to work out," say, "I'll do a 10-minute workout before bed."

2. The Most Common Excuses Are Easily Overcome

Time, age, fatigue, money, and talent are some of the most common excuses, yet they are all solvable. The truth is, successful people face the same challenges but choose to find solutions instead of making excuses.

ACTIONABLE EXERCISE

Identify your top three most frequent excuses. Write them down, and for each one, create a reframe statement. Example: Instead of "I don't have time to work on my goals," write, "I will prioritize 30 minutes a day for personal growth by waking up earlier or cutting down screen time." Commit to using your reframe statement every time the excuse tries to creep in.

3. **Commit to an "Excuse-Free Week"**

Eliminating excuses requires conscious effort. By challenging yourself to go one full week without making excuses, you train your mind to seek solutions instead of obstacles. This helps you build a new habit of ownership and action.

ACTIONABLE EXERCISE

For the next 7 days, every time you catch yourself making an excuse, stop immediately and write it down. Then, write the opposite action you could take instead. Share your challenge with a friend or accountability partner and check in with them daily. At the end of the week, reflect: how did eliminating excuses impact my actions, mindset, and results?

CHAPTER 23

You Cannot Do It Alone

arly on during my adult years, I was a big believer that if you want to succeed, you need to take care of everything yourself. Whatever task I was working on or the goal I was working towards, I always did it solo. I think a lot of that is our ego talking about how no one can do as good a job as we can, or it's a simple control issue of "I need to do everything myself." The truth is that you can never succeed at the highest level by yourself. There is no single success story out there that involves just one person. Even the best athletes, such as Michael Jordan, the late Kobe Bryant, and Tiger Woods, all had their own personal coaches and trainers they worked with. They had a team of people around them, including personal chefs, to ensure they ate the healthiest food for optimal performance.

The problem I see today with many older adults with unlimited potential is their fear of giving up control, thinking that no one can do it as well as them. The truth is that to scale your business and life, you need people on your team other than you. It's not easy to let go, but it is necessary. For clarity

I think it is important to understand going after your goals and dreams at first often will be a lonely process as discussed in Chapter 7, but once you gain some traction and strive to get to another level you physically cannot do it alone.

Today, I have a team of people I work with which I will share more about below. Still, the main reason I added this chapter is to hopefully encourage you that when you decide to go after your goals and dreams, trying to do it alone will limit your potential.

I remember vividly the day I hit one of the higher ranks within Beachbody, earning six figures a year and doing it all by myself. I gathered all the training, created online video training, made recognition photos, uploaded training calls to YouTube, hosted Zoom calls, and more. My strength was mentoring people through inspiration and empowerment. My weakness was all the administrative things that came with it. I once was told that if someone can do something 80 percent as good, they should outsource it. Why? So you can spend time on the things that you shouldn't outsource. For me, it was making videos and having personal one-on-one conversations with prospects. I couldn't have someone do that for me, but I could have them do all the other things. It was scary at first to ask for help, give up control, and question whether I could even afford it. But the truth is, by outsourcing many of my administrative duties, I freed myself up to do more things that would grow my business. That's when I hired my assistant, Tim, who is still with me today. I don't know where I would be without him. Our team and business would not have grown the way it did without Tim's help.

If you are building your own business early on, you may not be able to afford an assistant, and that's okay. At first, we do everything, but once you start having some success, part of being a successful entrepreneur is understanding when it's time to get help.

I am a big believer in life and business coaches. Yes, you can learn a lot by just using YouTube and Google, but I hired coaches multiple times in the last few years to help me with my business. I am not saying to do this, but when I decided to pursue being a speaker, I took the leap of faith and charged five figures on my credit card. You can learn through your own experiences, or you can leverage and learn through the experiences of others. This coach had been in the speaking industry for over 30 years. What would take me 5 years, I can learn from her in 5 months. Every single penny I spent with her came back to me tenfold. The best investment you can make in your life is in yourself. Investing money back into your business and, in this case, into yourself is worth every penny you spend doing it. Since I hired this first coach, I have hired five additional people to help me with my business. I will never stop investing money back into myself.

THE BEST INVESTMENT YOU CAN MAKE IN YOUR LIFE IS IN YOURSELF.

Maybe for you right now, it's just about getting your life in order. You are tired all the time, not healthy, and stressed all the time. This may be a perfect time to hire a life coach to help you formulate a plan to start thriving again. I have learned so much through my years in the state police, business, and speaking that I also decided to give back and coach people one-on-one. I believe in learning from those who have done it before you. Find someone who has what you want and learn from what they do. You can learn by working with them one-on-one.

I recently hired a nutritionist to help me with my diet as I train for my first ultramarathon. I know how to eat healthy, but properly fueling my body with the right amount and type of food became even more important. My nutritionist labeled me as a performance athlete and thus needed to be fueling my body as such.

Today, as a speaker, I work with a team of people. I still have Tim, but I also have an executive assistant, a data researcher, and an administrative assistant. They all play critical roles in my success today. I slowly added one at a time as my business grew. Please don't compare yourself to me and think you need all these people, too, but understand the importance of getting help as you grow. Don't be so blinded by your ego that you stunt your overall growth.

I also know people I am friends with who are business owners who clearly are floundering because they aren't willing to ask for help. I have even offered them help finding an assistant, but their ego is in the way. They agree with my suggestions but continue in their old ways a second later. Emails get missed. Deadlines pass. Schedules are getting messed up. This is all because of the unwillingness to ask for help. I then saw important issues only getting 50 percent effort and attention because this one person was trying to do it all. This doesn't work. Don't be the one to get in your own way.

There are two other people I need to mention in this chapter who are instrumental to my success. The first is my wife, Kristen. Having a supportive spouse is worth its weight in gold. I don't know how many times I bounce ideas off my wife, vent when I am struggling, or simply need to hear her say, "you are doing a good job, babe," which means the world to me. Furthermore, she takes care of our three kids when

I am traveling the road. We are a team, and my success is her success, too. When I have wins in my business or get a big booking, I often tell her, "We're doing it!" Not "I'm doing it." It's both of us, and I couldn't have succeeded without her.

I want to mention it wasn't always this way. I often hear about couples who have unsupportive spouses. More times than not, it's a communication breakdown because it was that way for me too. My wife despised all the time I spent on my phone when I started building my business. It wasn't until I sat her down and asked for her support and guidance that she came around. Include your spouse in what you do. Find a way to work together. What good is it if you are a public success and a private failure? It does no one any good if you are super successful in your career, but your home life is a mess. You want to excel in both areas. So be sure to take the time and find a way to make everyone happy.

Lastly, I would not be here today without my faith and belief in God. While it's not necessary to hold the same beliefs as me, take my experience as a sign to lean into the value system that works for you and the faith you need to find stillness. With that being said, for the last few years, my relationship with God has grown exponentially. Why? Because as I get older, the only thing that gives me a sense of peace, calm, and faith to keep going is God. As a Roman Catholic, going to church on Sundays is more than just sitting through mass. It's a way for me to reset my mind and my thoughts. Each morning, when I wake up and pray, it gives me a sense of peace and calm to thank God for everything I have and surrender the outcome of my success to something bigger than myself. I see God as the best teammate anyone can have.

I joined my parish's men's Bible study, which meets during Lent and Advent. Reading scripture and discussing it with others has become influential in my life. It brings God and Jesus to life. So many success books I have read teach principles that come right from the Bible. I recently joined the parish council to help at my church and community because I feel closer to God giving back. When I run and pass my church, I always stop to say a quick prayer outside at the foot of the church steps. When I see a beautiful sunrise or sunset, I think of God and thank him. Before I speak on stage, I say a prayer and then pray again when I am done, thanking God for the opportunity. I would not have this gift to speak without him. I am not telling you what you need to do, but I can say to you once I started incorporating God more into my life, it completely gave me a sense of trust and calm, knowing I have someone much more powerful than me in control looking out for my best interests. We have gotten so far away from even saying the word God in our country, but maybe it's time we start returning to our roots and how it all started. I believe there would be less problems in the world. Perhaps for you, it's a different type of spiritual relationship with the universe or religion, and that's great, too. The point I am making here is to stop trying to control everything and do everything yourself. Let go a little and surrender it to whatever you believe in. Have trust in guidance bigger than yourself.

In summary, you cannot accomplish anything significant in your life alone, so stop trying to do everything. Lean on

LET GO A LITTLE AND SURRENDER TO WHATEVER YOU BELIEVE IN. HAVE TRUST IN GUIDANCE BIGGER THAN YOURSELF.

others. Ask for help. Hire people to help you. Most importantly, give yourself grace along the way. No one is perfect, but we are all *one decision away* from making that change.

🔑 *Key Takeaways*

1. Success Requires a Team, Not Just Talent

No one achieves greatness alone. Even the best in the world – athletes, entrepreneurs, and leaders – have teams, mentors, and support systems to help them reach their full potential. Trying to do everything yourself will limit your growth and success.

ACTIONABLE EXERCISE

List your current goals and responsibilities. Identify tasks that are draining your time or outside your expertise. Ask yourself: Who could help me with these? Make a plan to delegate or seek assistance for at least one of these tasks in the next week — whether it's hiring someone, asking a mentor, or collaborating with a peer.

2. Let Go of Control and Trust the Process

Many people hesitate to seek help because of ego, fear of losing control, or believing no one can do the job as well as they can. However, by outsourcing tasks and trusting others, you free up time to focus on what truly moves the needle forward.

ACTIONABLE EXERCISE

Identify one task that someone else could do at least 80 percent as well as you. Delegate or out-source that task within the next week. Reflect after

7 days: Did it free up your time? Did the task still get done well? What did you learn from letting go?

3. **Lean on Faith and Trusted Support Systems**

Whether through faith, mentorship, or personal relationships, having a strong support system provides guidance, reassurance, and a sense of purpose. Success isn't just about achievement – it's about having the right people and beliefs to sustain you.

ACTIONABLE EXERCISE

Write down three people (or faith-based practices) that provide you with strength and encouragement. Schedule a time this week to connect with one of them — whether it's having a conversation, attending a faith-based event, or seeking guidance from a mentor. Afterward, reflect: how did this connection impact my mindset and motivation?

CHAPTER 24

Doors Will Open for You

The worst thing anyone can do is to stand still in life. It single-handedly is a detriment to your fullest potential. As T.S. Elliot said, "Only those who will risk going too far can possibly find out how far one can go." We try to map out our entire life and plan everything just how we want it, and soon enough, we find out how wrong we are. We need to learn to control the controllables. You have complete control over how you react in every situation and ultimately decide whether to act on your decisions or not. At the same time, I personally surrender the outcome to God, knowing he will not let me flounder or fail. I will still face tough times, but surrendering the outcome to God will give me a sense of peace. I truly believe if you do your part (putting in the work) God will do his. But the key is that you must make the one decision to take action so new opportunities can present themselves. Standing still gets you nowhere.

If I were a betting man on November 2, 1998, when I was sworn in as a New York State Trooper, I would have bet my entire salary and pension that I would be a New York State Trooper for the rest of my life. Being in law enforcement was my dream job, so once I attained it, there was absolutely nothing else in the world that I wanted to do. Well, luckily, I didn't make any bets like that because if I did, I would be a very broke man. In a million years, I would have never predicted that I would be doing what I am doing today. Even if someone told me back in 1998 that in 25 years, I would be a keynote motivational speaker traveling the country as an author, I would have laughed in their face. No way. No how. But clearly, God had other plans.

Looking back now, I am astounded at where my life took me. About 15 years ago, when my wife and I were in a lot of debt, struggling, physically not thriving, and our marriage not doing the greatest, all we wanted at that moment was to improve our current situation. That's all that mattered. We needed to figure out our finances and start caring for our relationship and health. That was the only decision I needed to address at that moment. The one decision to fix us. Sitting my wife down and talking to her about every thing I shared led to us agreeing that we would start exercising together in the early mornings before our kids got up. That conversation with my wife opened the door to an at-home P90X workout program we did together. Then, doing P90X together opened the door to a direct sales business opportunity with the parent company of P90X called Beachbody. We then made the one decision to walk through that door and pursue that business. A business that paid off six figures of our debt and became a million-dollar earner. A business that allowed my wife to leave teaching after 13 years to work from home and be with our three kids.

Making the decision to walk through that door to build this business opened up another door when I was asked to share my story and speak at Beachbody's quarterly events about my success. During this time, both speaking opportunities increased, and the audience grew from about 20 people to 20,000 in the NFL Super Dome. At this point in my life, I believe God revealed a gift I didn't know I had: the natural ability to be a public speaker.

As I spoke more, it aligned with the time in my state police career that I had the option to retire at the young age of 43 and receive full benefits. I truly believe none of this happened by accident. I was presented with another door to walk through and step into public speaking.

This was by far the scariest and most challenging step of my life, but I could step back and remind myself of a few essential principles of life that I have already grown through. First, growth is uncomfortable. There will never be a point in your life when an opportunity presents itself that won't involve a level of discomfort, uncertainty, fear, and self-doubt, to name a few. It is your tell-tale sign **YOUR DISCOMFORT IS SIMPLY LIFE STRETCHING YOU TO ANOTHER LEVEL OF YOUR LIFE.** you are precisely where you need to be. I would not be a speaker today if I hadn't made the decision to build a Beachbody business. You must decide to push through your current level of discomfort for life to reveal to you what's next. Your discomfort is simply life stretching you to another level of your life. Furthermore, growth precedes opportunity. Once you commit to growth more opportunities will be placed in your path. It begins with the *one decision* of being uncomfortable.

Second, looking back, I can see that each time I pushed through a certain level of discomfort, I was only preparing for what was coming next. I grew more. I became more. I was being prepared for the next opportunity. For example, as a business owner, learning to face rejection or losing a $100 sale on an exercise program prepared me for what it would take to succeed in the speaking industry. The stakes are much higher when it comes to success as a speaker.

Often, when something is presented to you, it doesn't make sense. But if you look back at your life today, you may understand why everything happened. It all lines up with where you are today. We don't see it at the moment, but we often see it after the fact. This is all about having faith and trust in God and your future.

The three main pillars of the One Decision Away philosophy are vision, a positive mindset, and a sense of urgency. Why? I truly believe that to succeed in life while applying my philosophy, you need all three pillars to create momentum. Furthermore, for doors to open for you, these three fundamentals must apply.

For one, you need to have a vision for your life. Too many people go through the motions every day. We walk around like zombies, just trying to survive. Each day is the same as the next. We live a life on repeat, and one day bleeds into the next. We often feel unfulfilled and burnt out. Why? Because we aren't growing. We have no vision! We have no goals. Some have dreams, but if we do, we haven't made the *one decision* to pursue them.

The number one source of fulfillment is progress. A vision for your life that you are actively working towards creates fulfillment. Let me give you a watered-down example when I say progress creates fulfillment. I know I mentioned this earlier on in my book, but it deserves repeating. Have you ever had a to-do list of errands you need to run, maybe on a Saturday or Sunday, and as you run your errands and begin to check and cross things off your list, you feel a sense of accomplishment? Yes! I'm sure you do. That's what I mean. Progress equals fulfillment, and fulfillment happens during that dopamine release. This is even more powerful on a larger scale when you cast a vision. If you stand still, no new doors will be presented to you.

The second is having a positive mindset. There is so much to discuss here, but to keep it simple, facing discomfort and being uncomfortable is something you just need to get used to. Learning to stay focused and keep a positive mindset during tough times and times of opportunity is the only way to level up and have more significant opportunities presented to you. Someone once told me, "David, you are exactly where you deserve to be." I didn't understand it at first, but looking back, the more I grew and the bigger goals I accomplished, the more it made complete sense.

Third is living with a sense of urgency. Procrastination gets you nowhere. As a matter of fact, each day you procrastinate, you end up in a worse spot, making it even harder to move forward. You need a sense of urgency in your life, or you will never see what you are capable of or what doors may be revealed to you.

In summary, yes, bigger doors will open for you, but without a vision, a positive mindset, and a sense of urgency, don't expect your next 30 days to look different from your last 30 days. You need to be the one to change – not your circumstances, but yourself.

God will then reveal to you what will come next, but you need to be the one to take action based on where you are right now. It's our job. I believe it's our duty and obligation to live up to our fullest potential and make the best of what we call "life." We only get one shot at it, so why not make it your best? We are all unique and have our own set of gifts and talents. It's our job to pursue them.

Here's a tip. If there is one word we need to overcome our self-doubt and fears so we can decide to take our next step, it's courage. We all have fear. No one is immune to it. Don't beat yourself up when you experience it. Give yourself some grace. You are not alone. But a little courage goes a long way; sometimes, it's all we need to push ourselves forward. Remember that word and anchor your mind to it when you face fear.

Your success is limitless. There is no cap on what you can do. We always have room to grow. So ask yourself: What if you actually did it? What if you hit that big, audacious goal? What if you actually blew your mind away with success? What if you landed that big job? Or succeeded at that crazy business idea? Now let me ask you this, what is the cost to your future self by not at least trying? Take a second to think about that. My friend, you have nothing to lose by trying. The worst case is you are right back to where you were when you started. You will survive. But remember, there are doors out there waiting to be opened. But it starts with deciding to walk through the one right in front of you.

For God to do his part, you need to do yours. You are the only person who can take action in your life. You need to make the *one decision*. You need to act and understand that taking action creates more opportunities. Doors will open for you like they have for me, and I can only imagine what doors will open for me next. But it starts with ourselves and what we decide to do today. Make the *one decision* today to improve your life so the next door can be revealed tomorrow – faith over fear.

⓷ Key Takeaways

1. Action Unlocks Opportunity

Standing still in life guarantees stagnation while taking decisive action creates momentum. Every opportunity you've had came from a single decision to move forward. Doors won't open unless you take the first step.

ACTIONABLE EXERCISE

Identify one decision you've been procrastinating on and take action today. It doesn't have to be a massive step — send the email, make the call, sign up for the class. Momentum starts with one small move.

2. Growth Requires Discomfort

Every new level of success brings discomfort, uncertainty, and fear. Instead of resisting these feelings, recognize them as signs that you're exactly where you need to be. Embracing discomfort is how you prepare for the next opportunity.

ACTIONABLE EXERCISE

Think about a time in your past when discomfort led to personal growth. Write it down, along with the lessons you learned. Now, apply that perspective to your current challenges and commit to taking the next step, even if it feels uncomfortable.

3. Vision, Mindset, and Urgency Are the Keys

For doors to open, you must have a clear vision, a positive mindset, and a sense of urgency. Without these three fundamentals, you risk staying stuck in the same place. Your success depends on the decisions you make today, not tomorrow.

ACTIONABLE EXERCISE

Set a 30-day vision for yourself. Write down a specific goal, along with daily actions that will move you toward it. Each morning, review your vision and take at least one action that aligns with it. This will train your mind to act with urgency and focus.

Conclusion

You are meant for greatness. You are meant to become more. You are meant to live up to your God-given potential. You are not meant to compare yourself to others, let fear stop you, or wake up each day just going through the motions. You are meant to feel fulfilled each day as you strive to be the best you can be.

Remember, keep it simple. Do not overcomplicate the choices and decisions you want to make. It's about making one decision at a time, and life will reveal to you what to do next. You know exactly what you need to do, and you already have everything you need to do it. Remember, it's different for everybody. Maybe it's to start taking care of your health. Maybe it's to apply for that new job. Maybe it's to start dating again. Maybe it's to start that new business. Maybe it's to write that book. I don't know what that is. Only you know. So, it's time to take that leap of faith, lean in, and make that *one decision.*

Everything up until this point in your life is in the past. It's finite. It's over. You are here. You must bless and release your past guilt, shortcomings, or successes. Your high school glory years are most likely over. It's time to create new ones.

What got you here will not get you to where you want to go tomorrow. It's what you need to do today that matters.

It doesn't matter if you are 20 years old or 100 years old. You have breath. You have fresh air. You have a heartbeat. You have God on your side. That means you still have time. This may be a page in your life. This may be a chapter in your life, but it's not the book of your life. Living the One Decision Away philosophy should apply to you right now, starting today.

Remember, this is your life. This is your journey, so do not compare your life to someone else's. We are all unique in our own ways and are meant to create and carve our own life's path. People won't support you at times, and that's okay. If it's in your mind, then it was put there for a reason. I believe God placed it there for you. That is the only sign you need to follow your heart with undeniable faith.

I spoke about many famous people who applied the One Decision Away philosophy to their lives. This is not some new way of living. It's a simple way to follow what you are destined to do. Yes, there will be obstacles along the way that we discussed in this book, such as feeling lonely, procrastination, fear, comparison, and living in the past, to name a few, but conversely, you have the tools now to overcome these obstacles, such as faith, vision, your why, principles over emotions, and patience. You can do this. It's not possible; it's past possible.

I want you to embrace this simple but powerful way of life. Wake up each day and proactively live your life to bring you closer to your dreams and goals – one decision at a time, one day at a time, one goal at a time. It's always only *one decision away.*

READY TO MAKE THE
ONE DECISION?

www.ingramcontent.com/pod-product-compliance
Lightning Source LLC
Chambersburg PA
CBHW070606130626
46556CB00001B/283